Bury St Edmunds
in the Great War

Dedication

Dedicated to my siblings Simon Cooper, Daryl Cooper, Troy Hoskin and Guy Beauchamp, with love and lots of memories, and to all the people of Bury St Edmunds who fought, suffered, died, endured or survived, especially to those who made the supreme sacrifice, in the Great War 1914–1918.

Your Towns and Cities in the Great War

Bury St Edmunds
in the Great War

Glynis Cooper

Pen & Sword
MILITARY

First published in Great Britain in 2017 by
PEN & SWORD MILITARY
An imprint of
Pen & Sword Books Ltd
47 Church Street
Barnsley
South Yorkshire
S70 2AS

ISBN 978-1-47383-401-9

A CIP catalogue record for this book is available from the British Library.

Typeset by Concept, Huddersfield, West Yorkshire HD4 5JL.
Printed and bound in England by CPI Group (UK) Ltd,
Croydon CR0 4YY.

Pen & Sword Books Ltd incorporates the imprints of Pen & Sword
Archaeology, Atlas, Aviation, Battleground, Discovery, Family History,
History, Maritime, Military, Naval, Politics, Railways, Select,
Social History, Transport, True Crime, and Claymore Press,
Frontline Books, Leo Cooper, Praetorian Press, Remember When,
Seaforth Publishing and Wharncliffe.

For a complete list of Pen & Sword titles please contact
PEN & SWORD BOOKS LIMITED
47 Church Street, Barnsley, South Yorkshire, S70 2AS, England
E-mail: enquiries@pen-and-sword.co.uk
Website: www.pen-and-sword.co.uk

Contents

Acknowledgments

I would like to acknowledge all the help and encouragement I have received in writing this book from family and friends; from local Bury St Edmunds historians Ron Murrell, Martin Taylor, Mark Cordell and David Addy; the West Suffolk Record Office; Roni Wilkinson, Matt Jones and the editorial team at Pen & Sword.

Introduction

Bury St Edmunds, set in the heart of the West Suffolk countryside, is a beautiful county town with a population of about 42,000 people. It boasts the ruins of an ancient abbey, with extensive and colourful gardens through which the River Lark meanders, Moyse's Hall – an early medieval merchant's house – several listed black and white timbered buildings, a unique Grade 1 listed Regency theatre, a rich history, and a profusion of legends.

The Angel Hotel was featured in *The Pickwick Papers* by Charles Dickens, who stayed in the hotel, and Daniel Defoe (author of *Robinson Crusoe* and *Moll Flanders*) was said to have lived for a while at Cupola House in the Traverse, almost next door to what is now the Nutshell, which is said to be the smallest pub in Britain. The town can trace its origins to Saxon times but takes its name from the East Anglian King Edmund, who was martyred by Danish Vikings in

Abbey ruins, Bury St Edmunds *c.*1922.

Abbey ruins, Bury St Edmunds.

Medieval timbered building, Bury St Edmunds.

Model of wolf guarding King Edmund's crown on roundabout near Southgate Street, Bury St Edmunds.

Abbot's Bridge, Bury St Edmunds *c.*1903.

AD869. After Edmund's death legend says that a wolf guarded his mortal remains until his followers found his body, and there is a sculpture, on Southgate Green roundabout in the town, of a 7ft (2.1m) high wooden wolf guarding a symbolic metal crown. The king was later canonised and popular legend says his body lies buried within the abbey grounds.

The abbey was founded in 1020 on the site of Edmund's shrine by the Benedictine Order, and it was one of the wealthiest in the country until the Dissolution of 1536. Street names today indicate the size of the abbey and its township through the number of original entrances: Northgate, Eastgate, Westgate, Southgate, Abbeygate, Churchgate, Raingate, Risbygate. However, Bury St Edmunds' chief claim to fame is that it was here, in the abbey, in 1214, that the barons met in secret to draw up Magna Carta, which King John was forced to sign at Runnymede the following year.

A French queen, who was also the great aunt of Mary, Queen of Scots, lies buried in St Mary's Church adjacent to the abbey. Mary Tudor, the younger sister of Henry VIII, was married to Louis XII of France and on his death she married her true love, Charles Brandon, Duke of Suffolk, in 1515. They had four children but their two sons died in childhood. Mary herself died prematurely in 1533 aged 37. Gibraltar Barracks was built in 1878 as the home of the Suffolk Regiment and latterly the Royal Anglian Regiment, but Bury St Edmunds has never really seen itself as a garrison town.

Date stone on Gibraltar Barracks, Bury St Edmunds.

Gibraltar Barracks, Bury St Edmunds.

The Barracks, Bury St Edmunds *c.*1912.

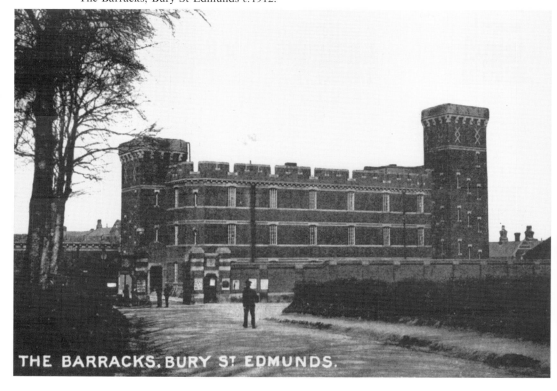

THE BARRACKS. BURY St EDMUNDS.

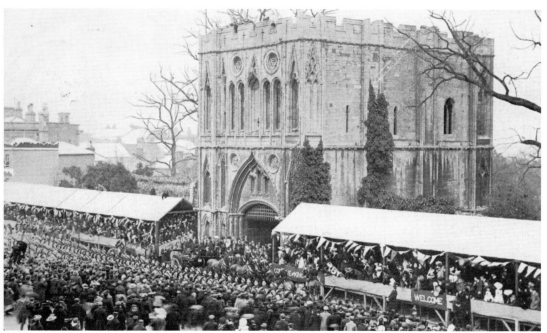

Visit of King Edward VII and Queen Alexandra to Bury St Edmunds in 1904.

Industries here centred on farming and wool for centuries, and although farming is still strong, brewing, sugar-beet processing and some engineering have joined the ranks. Today tourism is a major factor, but Bury St Edmunds remains essentially a working town with a strong sense of identity within the heart of an agricultural community.

CHAPTER 1

1914

The *Bury Free Press* was scarcely aware of the tense European situation in the summer of 1914. It was concerned with far more local affairs. Suffolk farm labourers' wages were among the lowest in the country and it was the problems with wages and conditions and tied cottages that occupied many column inches, along with proposals from the National Union of Farmworkers for improving the situation. The whole question of rural housing had recently been raised in the House of Commons by Sir Richard Winfrey MP. The town had originally been called St Edmundsbury, but this had proved to be a bit of a mouthful and over the centuries became Bury St Edmunds, often shortened to just Bury. After the Industrial Revolution this sometimes resulted in confusion with Bury in Lancashire, which caused some annoyance to the citizens of both towns.

The major annual event was the celebration of St Edmund, the long-dead sainted Saxon king buried within the abbey precincts. In the last week of July there was a service to commemorate the saint, and the Shrine of St Edmund's Procession left the cathedral, afterwards parading through the abbey grounds to the shrine of St Edmund. There were attendant harvest shows of fruit, flowers and vegetables, and there was a chirpy item on 'quoit notes' by someone calling themselves 'Discus'. Quoits, angling and fishing were the main sports in Bury at that time.

East Anglia usually has the driest and warmest summers in Britain and during the first week in August there were fêtes, regattas, weddings and sales of ram lambs, shearling ewes and the famous breed of Suffolk sheep, as townsfolk celebrated the long hot days of summer. The day before war was declared, Bury folk flocked to a large bank holiday fête held on Hardwick Heath.

Finally, on page 4 of the *Bury Free Press*, dated Saturday, 8 August 1914, international reality caught up with Bury St Edmunds. 'Europe at War! A gigantic struggle ...' screamed the headline. The paper then threw itself enthusiastically into responsible, detailed and comprehensive reporting of what had happened. In what, with hindsight, would prove to be one of the biggest understatements of all time, the paper declared:

> There is not the slightest cause for panic ... we want to keep calm, confident and courageous. Let us all unite in a sincere desire to help each other, and to sink all differences of opinion, and to be determined that we will act up to the best traditions of Britain ... [and] we shall come safely through the ordeal.

The paper then went on to say:

> All over the country the most intense interest is displayed in the terrible European war now raging ... but ... there is an absence of the unrestrained jingoism that marked the outbreak of the South African struggle ... [as] the horrors of sanguinary conflict are still fresh in the minds of British people.

However, no time was wasted in responding to the crisis. All military and naval leave in the area was immediately cancelled and a naval lieutenant due to marry in Bury on 6 August had his wedding postponed. The Territorials went into action immediately as health insurance was discussed for them and the Reserves in what, subsequently, might be termed 'a sick joke'. Page 5 of the newspaper was devoted to war and recruiting appeals and there were scenes of local mobilisation as the deputy mayor appealed for folk to remain level-headed and not panic. Collens Store, situated in Abbeygate Street, posted a large notice in its window proclaiming 'Our offer – food for the people!'

By the following week the war had been promoted to page 2 with a measured appeal to all the townsfolk:

> Slowly we are learning the terrible lesson which warfare among civilised nations teaches ... Keep calm, carry on and ensure that in future Kaiserism shall not have the power to wantonly deluge a continent in blood. Furthermore as Germany has a vast army and a strong navy then we may rely upon it that the end of the struggle is not yet.

Much of the country was still convinced that the war would be a short sharp lesson to the Germans and would be over by Christmas, but the

Bury Free Press was not so easily fooled. Just eleven days after war had been declared, the newspaper realised it was not going to be over any time soon.

Meanwhile, the ladies of Bury St Edmunds had already begun making garments for the troops and assisting the Red Cross, whose Bury headquarters were in Guildhall Street. St Michael's College was used as a centre for the working parties making garments. Suffolk Women's Voluntary Aid Detachment (VAD), whose commandant had the unfortunate name of Dr Stiff, were also involved in caring duties. North Hill House on Northgate Street and Mustow House were converted into hospitals. Bury St Edmunds boy scouts patrolled main trunk and telephone wires to keep lines of communication open and acted as orderlies at the Suffolk Regiment depot. Bury St Edmunds Rifle Range offered free use of the range for the duration of the war. The Suffolk Yeomanry (the Loyal Suffolk Hussars) were given a rousing send-off from Angel Hill as they marched off to war, and the 3rd Suffolk Battalion made an early morning departure from Bury St Edmunds.

Local churches held special intercessionary services for the war. 'The county of Suffolk,' thundered the *Bury Free Press*, 'has done its duty in supplying officers and men to uphold England's honour at the seat of war ... with patriotism and zeal ...' Some did even more.

Angel Hill, Bury St Edmunds *c.*1911.

ANGEL HILL, BURY ST. EDMUNDS.

A lady from Haverhill in Suffolk had her husband, five brothers and a brother-in-law leave for active service while Thetford, 10 miles away from Bury, just across the Norfolk border, earned acclaim from the paper:

> Look at gallant little Thetford which has contributed 10% of its total population to the fighting ranks of Britain.

Then, addressing the Home Front:

> Now it remains for those left at home to play their part in preparing to render assistance to the wounded who may be landed upon our shores.

It was at this point that a tale of Eastern magic, romance and tragedy touched the town. For over a quarter of a century an Indian prince had served with the Suffolk Yeomanry, and subsequently with the neighbouring Norfolk Yeomanry, rising from the rank of second lieutenant to that of major. Prince Frederick Duleep Singh was the second son of the last Maharaja of the Punjab, Duleep Singh, and he grew up at the family home in the village of Elveden, on the Suffolk border, 10 miles from Bury.

Duleep Singh had been separated from his mother as a boy and brought to exile in Britain after the annexation of the Punjab in 1849. He was then made to present his birth-right of the fabulous Koh-i-Noor diamond to Queen Victoria. Prince Freddie, as he was known, had retired from the army in 1909, but he lost no time in re-joining his regiment and volunteering for active service when the Great War broke out. He loved England and, whatever his private feelings about the way the British had treated his father, he was completely loyal to the English crown, but he did not forget his Sikh heritage. In woodlands bordering the grounds of his home, a fourteenth-century manor house some 17 miles from Bury St Edmunds, he built a small Indian temple. Set back from the road and hidden by trees it was a quiet, pretty and lonely spot where he and his sister, Princess Bamba, could pay secret homage to their lost homeland.

Prince Freddie had no children and today there are only folk memories left of him. His house, where Virginia Woolf began her writing career in 1906, has been converted to luxury holiday apartments, and the remains of his temple lie hidden under a thick carpet of lily of the valley.

The Defence of the Realm Act (DORA) was passed on 8 August. The Act basically allowed the government and military authorities to take whatever action they considered necessary for security or the successful defence of the country. Initially this covered censorship, commandeering of food, supplies or horses for the troops, and restrictions on the use of fuel and lighting. Lesser activities like flying kites, lighting bonfires and feeding bread to wild animals, were forbidden as well. A number of Bills were also passed to enable more free meals for feeding schoolchildren and war pensions for civilians and widows, as well as a Housing Bill for the purpose of building workmen's houses all over the country.

There were rumours of food shortages, but Suffolk's lord lieutenant made an appeal for calm and common sense. There was, he said, 'No occasion for panic. There is plenty of food and gold and definitely no shortage of Bird's custard or Horniman's tea.' By the end of September, Lyons and Liptons (both tea-trading companies) were engaged in a huge libel case after Liptons had alleged that some members or directors of Lyons were German and that purchase of their goods was helping Britain's enemies. There was also a proposal for the early closing of pubs, which was giving folk the jitters. The Corn Exchange was transformed into a centre of entertainment for the troops, providing a reading and writing room, free games and refreshments. The YMCA followed suit and set-up an entertainments tent in a meadow on Fornham Road, and they were supported by the Railway Mission Hall on the same road doing the same thing.

Kitchener's call to arms for recruiting members for the British Expeditionary Force was now under way and a recruiting drive in Bury was progressing quite successfully, with Lord Stradbroke giving recruitment speeches in the Corn Exchange and making pleas for men to join the colours. The local education committee offered to provide evening classes in the camps for recruits. Enthusiastic young men from all walks of life signed-up and it was also noted that no able-bodied men remained in the local workhouse. In addition, volunteers were needed for the Cyclist Battalion of the Suffolk Regiment.

The Third Suffolks were engaged in France for several weeks before returning to Felixstowe. By early September, the first casualties of the Suffolk Regiment had come back to the town with 'thrilling stories of fighting at the Front', and it was reported that 'the gallant Suffolks were still up to strength'. The sum of £82.14s.6d (£7,090) was collected for hospitals in Bury and local ladies had made

100 shirts and knitted 100 pairs of socks for the Suffolks by mid-September. The news was full of 'great victories for the Allies and great losses for the enemy', but there were reports of prolonged fighting and a Bury St Edmunds vicar commenting on the war said that it was 'the most awful harvest of slaughter'. A number of Belgian refugees fleeing the German occupation of Ghent arrived in the town with stories to tell of appalling atrocities. They were initially accommodated in Hardwick House and cared for by the townspeople.

The Suffolk branch of the Soldiers and Sailors Families Association was kept busy and so were the County and Poor Relief organisations. So far, £368.16s.5d (£31,610) had been raised for the Bury St Edmunds National Relief and Local Distress Fund, and West Suffolk County War Relief Fund had raised £6,517.3s.7d (£558,600). There was hardship as the separation allowances paid to wives and families when the breadwinners were away fighting were woefully inadequate. Soldiers' wives received between 12s.6d (£55) and 23s (£104+) per week, depending on their husband's rank, plus 5 shillings (£22) for the first child and 3s.6d (£15+) for the second child. A further 5/- (£22) per week was paid to the wives of each surviving Bury Corporation employee who was away fighting, although this was usually deducted from the separation allowance.

Food and fuel prices were rising steadily and rents were going up, despite the war and the decline in individual circumstances. As in most other towns, a number of inhabitants were doubling up together because, with their men folk away, some families could not afford the increased rents. The Borough Medical Officer, Dr Stork, an equally unfortunate name to that of Dr Stiff, prepared a report on the quality and quantity of the housing in the town, but the council declined to investigate because they didn't want the resulting expense, although it was eventually promised that 'some steps would be taken'. Coupled with this was the ongoing problem of agricultural labour and tied cottages. A wage of 15/- (£66) for a 65 hour week and often sub-standard accommodation was not an attractive proposition and, besides, it meant that many rural cottages were effectively taken out of the general housing market, which had an adverse effect on country towns like Bury St Edmunds. Enlisting was now causing a shortage of agricultural labour and West Suffolk Education Committee met in Bury St Edmunds to discuss the possibility of replacing farm labourers with boys over the age of 12 who would already have homes with their own families.

It was around the end of October that the *Bury Free Press* decided to run a weekly 'patriotic farming' column. 'Agricultural motors' (tractors) were being promoted due to an ongoing lack of horses and labour as a result of the war. The amount of capital investment needed for tractors was proving a problem, but it was a powerful argument that a tractor could be used for ploughing, cultivation and cartage, which would save many man-hours of work. There was also a recognition that the British sugar-beet industry needed encouragement and assistance. A hefty £11,000-worth (£968,000) of sugar and sugar-beet had been imported from Germany before the war, and that lost trade gave British farmers an opportunity for enterprise that would continue to be profitable even after the war was over. Suffolk had thousands of acres that could be utilised for such purpose. Then, as now, the British public were fond of their sugar, and it eventually became the first foodstuff to be rationed.

'Patriotic farming' also advised that sensible stock feeding of their animals was required from farmers. Linseed cake was expensive, while coconut cake was much cheaper. However, always wary of change, British farmers were suspicious of the cheaper feeds used by their continental counterparts. Bury St Edmunds had a large cattle market and British meat may have been of better quality, but the war situation called for drastic measures and new economies. Leaves were to be collected for compost heaps and extra care was to be taken of root and vegetable seeds. Cultivation of potatoes was still secondary to wheat crops for farmers, but they came to be of prime importance for allotment growers. British farming had had a troubled century, which included two depressions and a brief golden age. The first depression, which lasted from 1813–1830, was due to a slump in farming prices as a result of unstable finances, high taxation, discharged soldiers and unemployment in the peace following the Napoleonic Wars. The worst years were 1814–1816, which saw many farmers go bankrupt and large tracts of land abandoned.

Arthur Young, an English agricultural writer who lived in Bradfield Combust near Bury, helped to bring about agricultural reforms and the golden age, from 1837–1862, followed the discovery of artificial fertilisers, the development of modern drainage systems, the invention of new machinery and implements, and the use of steam power.

The second depression, 1874–1914, was a result of foreign competition and cheaper corn plus the new ability to freeze meat for carriage across the world. Subsequently, many of the larger estates were maintained as game reserves for hunting and shooting parties. 'Horn up, corn down' was a popular contemporary summary of the situation. Thus, by the time the Great War started, farming was not in a good place with hundreds of thousands of arable acres neglected. Suffolk was seriously affected, like other places, but it had a lower density of population than many other counties and since medieval times wool had been the staple commodity for the region.

Bury St Edmunds, as the county and main market town for West Suffolk, held regular sheep and horse fairs alongside its weekly cattle market (which lasted until well into the second half of the twentieth century), and local home-grown produce was sold in the town's food markets.

Bury also had a thriving agricultural engineering industry. Robert Boby had started an ironmongers on St Andrews Street, which became a leading manufacturer for grain dressing and winnowing machines for corn, seed and malt as well as producing hay makers, seed drills and various field equipment. Boby died in 1886, but his company continued to prosper and was still doing well by the time of the Great War, when the government decided that some manufacturing bases should be given over to the production of munitions. Boby's Works was the first to be commandeered in Bury followed by T.H. Nice, who had a garage works on Abbeygate Street.

Marketplace, Bury St Edmunds *c.*1915.

Market Place, Bury St. Edmunds.

Ampton Hall, Bury St Edmunds *c.*1901.

Bury St Edmunds had gained a reputation during the monastic period (*c.*1100–1536) as a 'spital place' where monks from the abbey tended the sick in a half-dozen small hospitals around the town. Most of the old stone-built little hospices were long gone by the early twentieth century, but the town retained its medical reputation. Suffolk General Hospital (as it was then known) on Hospital Road, was initially established in 1825 in a converted military depot (redundant since Waterloo). The hospital was helping to care for wounded troops alongside temporary Red Cross hospitals within the town, especially on Northgate Street, as well as those in the halls of nearby villages, notably Hardwick House, Ampton Hall in Ickling-ham and Hengrave Hall. In 1914 the Isolation Hospital (located on Sicklesmere Road, but which no longer exists) was let to West Suffolk County Council by Thingoe Rural District Council to be run on military rather than district lines.

Smallpox remained a threat, an epidemic of scarlet fever had just run its course, and there was an outbreak of mumps, but the main problem was returning troops with infectious diseases, especially sexually transmitted ones. Tuberculosis was also still a big problem, but this was being addressed by the Bury St Edmunds and West Suffolk Sanatorium (the building still exists) on Southgate Street.

Despite the war, Bury St Edmunds was not giving up on its festivities just yet. In November, the serious traditional ceremony of mayor-making was observed. This ceremony was common to many towns but several towns, especially in the north, had curtailed their mayor-making ceremony for 1914. Bury St Edmunds, however, had another even more important event to celebrate because 20 November was the 700th anniversary of the drawing up of Magna Carta. The barons of England, upset that King John was seeking to erode their rights under the Coronation Charter of Henry I issued in 1100, met secretly in the abbey at Bury St Edmunds to draw up a charter of laws and civil liberties. It was a time of unrest and spies were everywhere. Pretending that they were visiting the shrine of St Edmund in the abbey grounds on the saint's feast day (20 November) so as not to arouse suspicion, the barons swore on the high altar of the Church of St Edmund that they would unite to force King John to sign their great charter restoring the laws and liberties that were under threat and which laid down the principle that no one was above the law, not even the king or queen. The king had finally agreed to sign the charter seven months later on 15 June 1215 at Runnymede. Much was made of the anniversary, with church services and a procession, the towns-folk perhaps feeling it was ironic that it should have occurred in the year that a foreign power was doing its best to erode 'liberty, equality and fraternity' in the country.

The Bird and Tree Challenge Shield was also due to be presented soon with great ceremony.

The idea of the shield was an attempt by the Royal Society for the Protection of Birds (RSPB), particularly in rural areas, to encourage the interest of young people in birds, trees and habitats, which would hopefully increase protection for birds by preventing vandalism and the resulting loss of nests, eggs and sites. Teams of children from local schools were registered as RSPB cadets. Each cadet would select a bird and a tree for observation during the year and would keep notes and descriptions, as well as record events that occurred concerning their chosen bird or tree. At the end of the study period the cadet had to write separate report essays on his/her bird and tree. The six best essays (on three birds and three trees) were then entered into the competition. Subsequently the County Challenge Shield, certificates, medals and book prizes were awarded according to merit by RSPB judges and winning was considered to be a great local honour.

The town was determined not to let the war spoil Christmas for this year. Despite staffing shortages caused by enlisting, which had resulted in the introduction of lunchtime closing for some shops and curtailed the opening hours of certain banks, by the end of November a number of local stores were promoting Christmas shopping and present-buying. Collens' store was advertising special Christmas fruits, and Raphael Tuck had issued a new set of Christmas cards, which were proving very popular with the townsfolk. There was also an increase in weddings as local soldiers and sailors wanted to spend some precious married life with their sweethearts, whom they might well never see again. The Theatre Royal put on a special Christmas performance in aid of the war and raised £62 (just over £5,300). The Queen's Work for Women Fund raised £20 (£1,760) through coin collections for local assistance. A sale at Long Melford raised £147.17s (£12,670) for the Belgian Relief Fund, and the Bury St Edmunds national relief and local distress funds raised £693.14.9d (£59,460) by the end of the year.

Increased taxes on tea and sugar, however, somewhat dampened the festive food spirit. There had long been import taxes on both commodities but the increased duty on tea from 21 November hit hard, especially for poorer folk. It had gone up from 5d (£1.85) to 8d (£2.93), so that a pound (500kg) of tea now cost 1s 6d (£6.60). During the war total taxation would rise from 6.5 per cent to 30 per cent, which, then as now, affected those on low wages and the poorest in society the most. There were fears that increases in the costs of coal and the carriage of goods would force prices up even more. Nevertheless, there was much good Christmas fare for the Suffolks, food and gifts for local soldiers and sailors; and appeals were launched for cigarettes, pipes and tobacco for the troops; although Princess Mary also sent each serving soldier and sailor a gift of 'ciggies, a pipe and baccy'. 'A Soldier of the King' recruitment campaign was underway in the town, appealing for new recruits to take the place of those who had been wounded, and concerns of invasion were already being expressed.

In the last edition of the paper for 1914, the *Bury Free Press* tried to be upbeat and restore a little semblance of the normality that had been swept away when war was declared. The paper insisted that the children's Christmas had not been spoiled at all, printing lots of cheerful news about local events, festivities and parties, church services and carol concerts, concluding with notes on pike fishing and warnings against chilblains. The year ended with floods and gales, and the River Lark threatened to burst its banks, but Bury folk tried their best to keep their spirits up as they wished each other a happy new year. No one had any idea of the terrifying forces that were about to be unleashed upon them.

CHAPTER 2

1915

January was a miserable month, cold, wet and windy. The River Lark burst its banks and the River Stour flooded as well. An outbreak of diphtheria occurred in the nearby town of Haverhill, causing much local alarm, while Bovril was seen as both prevention and cure for influenza. The question of lighting was still causing difficulties and shops were ordered to close earlier – by 8.00pm Monday to Friday and 10.00pm on Saturdays. The War Office issued advice that perishable foods should not be included in parcels for soldiers overseas. The Christmas parcels had, in several cases, resulted in some misfortune.

Moyse's Hall set up a Roll of Honour and intercession services were held in local churches. There were Zeppelin raids on the Norfolk coastal towns of Yarmouth, Cromer and Sheringham. This was a terrifying new aspect to war. It was the first use of aerial warfare, when death and destruction literally rained from the skies, and citizens realised they were no longer safe in their own country even if there was no enemy occupation. It was a sober and frightening thought. In an attempt to be pragmatic, Bury folk tried to focus attention on actual problems on the ground rather than on potential problems in the skies.

As within the teaching profession, shortage of labour due to enlistment was now causing real problems for agriculture, and workers on the land felt 'that the industry was treated unfairly and farm hands were looked down upon'. The Bury medical officer of health reported again on the sub-standard housing in both the borough and the surrounding countryside. He believed it necessary that 'the working classes should be properly and comfortably housed'. Local councillors agreed in principle. In practice, however, there was the question of war economies, and they didn't want to inflict hardship on property owners even though some of those owners were, in turn, inflicting hardship on already impoverished families. There was also discussion of a Suffolk-based scheme for village milling, with proposals that a 'midget miller plant' might be installed in each village to enable the tenant farmers to produce flour from home-grown wheat that would 'allow normal low prices of bread for the poor' during the war.

A 'meat or wheat' debate concerning the use of arable land was already underway. The patriotic farming column in the *Bury Free Press* advocated co-operation between groups of half-a-dozen farmers for the purchase of motor ploughs and 'lurries' to lessen the need for manpower. Crops of parsnips were to be encouraged because they were utilised as food for both people and animals. Spring vetches could be used as a 'catch crop' to renew soils and their nutrients and the use of Irish labourers was advocated. But it was agreed that medium loam soils should remain permanent pasture for livestock or the cutting of hay. Meadows growing Italian rye grass, cow-grass, foxtail and white clover would be ideal for this purpose. In addition there was a campaign to grow sugar-beet so that the choice of land use would become 'meat, wheat or beet'. The Anglo-Netherland Sugar Corporation was offering a sliding scale of prices and profitable sugar-beet growing hints, and Dutch and Belgian labour could be used for sugar-beet cultivation. Besides, there was the bonus of gaining the trade lost by Germany. There were also those who argued that now was the time to capture the foreign market for eggs.

Bury St Edmunds had no labour exchange, so at the end of March local farmers were asked for their labour requirements until September. Men and boys were needed for ploughing, harvesting, dealing with the horses, and heavy work. More liberally (or realistically) minded than their more northern counterparts, Suffolk farmers also required female labour for milking, dairy and poultry work, weeding corn, and preparation of peas and turnips for market gardens. Workers would then be supplied by the Suffolk Labour Committee.

Strong recruitment campaigns were organised and the pressure to enlist increased. The *Bury Free Press* now devoted at least one, sometimes two, of its broadsheet pages per week to war news and casualties. The Bury Volunteer Training Corps appealed for more members but could not obtain the council funding necessary to raise its membership from 160 to 230.

The presence of the 1st Suffolks in France had been welcomed. The 5th Suffolks were at Thetford, and efforts were being made to raise another battalion in West Suffolk. Bakers and butchers were urgently

Suffolk Regiment or Yeomanry Crown Street Bury St Edmunds *c.*1915. (courtesy of Martyn Taylor)

required for the Army Service Corps. News of the Dardanelles attack prompted one Bury soldier to quip that 'soon it would be moving day for the Kaiser', dismissing the Germans as 'pirates'. As well as the heavy fighting in the Dardanelles during the Gallipoli campaign, there had also been heavy fighting in the French town of Ypres, and in late April lethal chlorine gas was unleashed by the Germans against the Allies for the first time during the Second Battle of Ypres.

There were appeals for binoculars for the Suffolks, although no one was quite sure why the War Office didn't supply these items as part of basic equipment. A number of troops, around 3,000 in total, were billeted in Bury, which benefitted local trades, bars and social life, especially afternoon promenades in the Abbey Gardens. The number of Red Cross hospitals in and immediately around the town had increased to twelve, including Elveden Hall where Prince Freddie had grown up.

On the night of 29/30 April, the townsfolk of Bury St Edmunds got the shock of their lives. They were attacked by a Zeppelin. Although DORA regulations of lighting were clear, people in Bury had not been very conscientious about adhering to the restrictions and in the panic that ensued, with bombs raining down on the town centre, individual house lights were switched on and Bury shone like a beacon in

Zeppelin incendiary bombs dropped on Bury St Edmunds, 30 April 1915. (courtesy of Martyn Taylor)

the night. Captain Eric Linnarz could steer his aircraft simply by following the blazing trail of lights. It didn't help matters that the night was clear with bright moonlight.

Zeppelin LZ.38 was 536ft (162.5m) long with four engines and 2 tons of bombs, it carried a crew of twenty-two and could travel at 60mph (105km). The Zeppelin had already attacked Yarmouth and Ipswich before following the route of the A45 to Bury. Forty-one incendiary shells and four high explosive bombs were dropped on and around the town but, astonishingly, the only casualties were a border collie killed by debris in the Buttermarket and a few hens on an allotment. However, there was a great deal of structural damage. There are several eye-witness accounts, including descriptions from three Red Cross VAD workers as they returned home from the Suffolk General Hospital just after midnight, which give some good detail:

> Our attention was attracted by a strange noise ... like a train ... but it was an airship right over us all ... as we got to the bottom of Mill Road and into King's Road we saw the bombs drop from the Zeppelin. (Red Cross workers.)

> I was lying awake when I heard the whirl of an airship ... I dressed and went down into the street and saw the machine

coming in over Moyse's Hall ... it then veered towards the Park [Abbey Gardens] and seemed to change its course ... coming straight back again and dropping bombs on the way ... in the sky over the railway station I noticed a particularly brilliant light. I am certain it was a Zeppelin. (Tailor in the Buttermarket.)

The Zeppelin ... looking like a monster cigar ... attacked Moreton Hall at 12.30 midnight then moved to Northgate [railway] Station ... in Northgate Avenue it blew up a tree near the East Anglian School ... then hit Whitmore's timber yard and Aetna Road before destroying the Anchor pub opposite Looms Lane ... incendiaries hit 8 Angel Hill, Day's boot and shoe shop, and numbers 30–33 in the Buttermarket ... four premises were damaged between the Suffolk Hotel and the Half Moon pub before St Andrew's Street and King's Road were attacked ... where St Andrew's auction rooms were hit and the stables set on fire ... and Boby's Engineering Works on St Andrew's Street was also damaged ... Westley village on the outskirts of Bury was the last to be hit before the Zeppelin flew off in the direction of Woolpit. (Account of the attack pieced together from a number of different sources.)

Zeppelin raid damage in the Buttermarket Bury St Edmunds, 30 April 1915. (courtesy of Martyn Taylor)

Zeppelin raid damage in Northgate Street, Bury St Edmunds, 30 April 1915.

The local newspapers had a field day with headlines after the attack. 'Aerial visitation of the baby killers!' thundered one, while another went for sarcasm with 'Typical Hun bravery!' and a third searched for some humour with 'Bomb assault on chickens!' Amazingly, no one had been killed or injured but there was considerable damage to property and businesses. Visitors flocked to Bury so they could see the damage caused and talk of it in horrified whispers over cups of tea in local cafés. Troops billeted nearby helped to save horses during the attack, and the fire brigade was highly praised for its work while the mayor spoke proudly of the 'splendidly calm demeanour of the inhabitants', but he 'never wanted another twenty minutes like it'. Serious reductions were now made in light at night so that, generally, any lighting was 'very subdued'. Public lamps were not lit and some-one trying to walk the Bury pavements in the dark described the experience as 'like playing a game of blind man's buff' (a children's game which involved finding people by touch and not sight).

A week later the sinking of the *Lusitania* caused tempers to flare in the town. The Royal Navy had refused to allow goods to be shipped to Germany from the United States, which at that time was neutral. Declaring all cargo in neutral waters to be contraband, the navy seized the shipments. In retaliation, Germany established a sub-marine blockade around Britain aimed at sinking all merchant ship-ping connected with the British Isles. In the first few months of 1915,

Aftermath of Zeppelin attack, Bury St Edmunds 1915.

over ninety ships were destroyed and this began to cause shortages of certain commodities. Then, on 7 May, the Germans caused international outrage by torpedoing and sinking the *Lusitania* off the Old Head of Kinsale in County Cork. Over 1,200 people drowned. The Germans argued that the ship was carrying arms, a claim hotly refuted by the British and American authorities. Unfortunately, a hundred years after the event, diving teams and research have proved the German accusations to be correct. Nevertheless, in 1915 it caused a huge backlash of public opinion against anyone or anything German in origin and there were a number of anti-German riots all over Britain.

In Bury St Edmunds the landlord of the Griffin on the corner of Cornhill and Brentgovel Street was called Theodore Jacobus. He was, in fact, a British citizen, but on 15 May, a week after the sinking of the *Lusitania*, the pub was attacked by angry locally billeted Royal Engineers and bricks were thrown through the windows. Two days later, West Suffolk County Council dismissed its weights and measures inspector, Mr Walters, from its town offices simply because he had German parents. Braham's scrap merchants in Risbygate Street were forced to take out advertisements to prove that they had no German blood in them, and the King of Prussia pub on the corner of Prussia Lane and Southgate Street was hastily renamed the Lord Kitchener.

The *Bury Free Press* reported yet another national tragedy on 22 May. This was the Quintinshill rail disaster near Gretna Green, a train crash involving five trains and resulting in the deaths of 230 people and 246 serious injuries. To this day it holds the record for being the worst railway disaster in British history. One of the trains was a troop train with old wooden carriages and gas lighting. The troop train hit a local train, which had stopped, and both trains were then hit by the London–Glasgow sleeper. After the crash, the gas lights set fire to the wooden carriages and a fierce inferno ensued, which engulfed all five trains, two of which were in adjacent sidings. Nearly all the dead were Scottish soldiers on the troop train, but there were also four children who have never been identified. Bury folk were shocked and horrified. There were two stations in the town and the Zeppelin raid had taken place only three weeks beforehand. Such a tragedy could so easily have happened to them as well.

The Whitsuntide Festival arrived and Bury St Edmunds folk wanted to try and push thoughts of war to the back of their minds. It proved difficult to do, however, and controversy was immediately caused when a brilliantly lit fair was set up next to the railway station. This prompted a touch of nostalgia for yesteryear from one of the local paper's readers. She wrote of:

> Whitsun flowers with romantic sounding names such as king cups, cuckoo flowers, buttercups and colts' foot, and the cherry, apple and pear blossoms. Village wines, home-made from parsnips; cowslips; dandelion; damson; redcurrant; rhubarb; sloe; gooseberry and others cheered festival celebrations; and there would be plum cakes and custard for friends, as well as beautiful custards, stewed prunes and gooseberry fools. Afterwards simple games and dancing to the village fiddler.

Sadly, she concluded, 'times, seasons, manners and customs are all altered.'

There were the usual church services held in the Cathedral and St Mary's, and there was a scouts' camp at Saxham, but everyone knew it just wasn't the same at all.

Memorial to those who fell in France and Flanders in the Great War, St Mary's Church, Bury St Edmunds.

WW1 Cenotaph for the Suffolk Regiment in St Mary's Church, Bury St Edmunds
*c.*1938.

In an attempt to provide additional employment and to take advantage of trade lost by Germany as a result of the war, the toy-making industry in England enjoyed a revival. Before the war there had been nearly half a million toy imports from Germany. By 1915 this had dropped dramatically to just over 1,000 before petering out altogether by 1918. Imports from France, America and Japan made up some of the shortfall, but an opportunity was seen, especially by organisations like the Primrose League, to create a new cottage industry that would provide employment for women and older children. Local housewives and a number of West Suffolk schools took part in the initiative, which proved quite successful until the austerity of the economy and, post-1918, men returning from the war made such projects unprofitable. Toy soldiers for boys and nicely dressed dolls for girls were among the most popular items.

A large acreage of farmland had been used to grow buckwheat or kidney vetch, which provided food and cover for game, but large numbers of the 'hunting, shooting and fishing' fraternity had now joined the colours so that such game reserves had become largely redundant, and there was a call for cultivation on the old four year cycle of:

1. wheat or rye
2. root crops
3. barley or oats
4. seed and flocks of sheep (which here, in Suffolk, meant black-faced highly valued Suffolk sheep)

Farming was still of paramount importance to Bury St Edmunds and its surrounding villages, but agricultural labour was in short supply due to enlistment. Matters weren't helped when, in its patriotic farming column, the *Bury Free Press* commented that amateur help could be a hindrance if it disrupted farm routines or was not prepared to work all hours in all weathers. Suffolk farmers, like Cambridgeshire farmers, Cheshire farmers, and farmers all over the country, were determined to try and bring their sons home from the Front to work the farms. They totally failed to recognise the potential value of female labour, refusing to even think about training women. Farmers also doggedly refused prisoner-of-war labour, which irritated the government because the Germans had no scruples about using English prisoners-of-war on their farms, as well as refusing Irish labourers who 'cost too much', and offers of help from boy scouts who were deemed too young and inexperienced. How difficult could it be to sow and reap with reasonable success? argued government ministers, when whole families had been doing it since the Stone Age. There was also the problem of very low agricultural wages. This deterred a fair numbers of possible applicants, who took jobs in transport, munitions, council departments, even shops, that were better paid.

After the winter floods there was a drought, which eventually ended in torrential thunderstorms, and 'Bury sparrows were feasting on barley crops'. Imported eggs were now unavailable, so there was a high demand for English laid eggs and, as well as farmers and smallholders, cottagers were being encouraged to keep hens. Smallholders were told that sunflower seeds were a good profitable line of produce.

The 'patriotic farming' columns of the *Bury Free Press* warned farmers against paying high prices for the low quality manures that were being touted around as fertilisers, adding that rotation of crops for 'strong land' could be six-fold, revitalising the soil with goodness as each crop grown would give and take different nutrients. Suggestions for a six-crop rotation included:

1. turnips, swedes, cabbages and mangolds
2. wheat
3. beans or clover (in alternation)
4. wheat
5. beans or clover (in alternation)
6. wheat

However, there was a campaign to cultivate sugar-beet in the UK and the farming land around Bury St Edmunds was ideal. There was a high demand for preserving sugar to make jams and jellies from locally grown fruit, and English people had a sweet tooth. Before the war, 1,600,000 tons of sugar had been imported annually from Germany. This trade was now lost but it had created a new opportunity for British farmers. Traditionally, cane-sugar was preferred. In 1840, cane-sugar accounted for 95 per cent of sugar consumption, and beet-sugar for just 5 per cent. In 1914, with the war raging and the Germans mounting assaults on British merchant shipping, beet-sugar accounted for 54 per cent of consumption. The Great Eastern Railway Company, eager to co-operate, offered cheap and efficient transport for sugar to encourage Suffolk farmers to grow the crop. Bury St Edmunds eventually became a centre for the refinement of sugar from beet-sugar, and remains so to the present day (2016).

Life in the country was deemed to be healthier than urban life. Infant mortality was 105 per 1,000 in rural areas whereas in industrial towns it could be as high as 440 per 1,000. However, cottage accommodation in the villages and on the farms was of poor standard. The village of Mildenhall in Suffolk was censured for 'uninhabitable cottages', but a local councillor blamed the inhabitants saying that they were simply afraid of fresh air. Overcrowding remained a problem. Rents were still rising and many families whose men folk were away fighting had little option but to put their furniture and possessions into storage and double-up with other family members.

Tuberculosis remained a prolific disease and epidemics of measles, mumps, scarlet fever and influenza spread rapidly in cramped conditions. Due to the war there was a shortage of medicines, which caused prices to rise, and the poorer families suffered the most. Hygiene and education in family care were important. Sunlight Soap promoted itself in an advertising campaign, including military allusions of use, with the slogan 'Cheerfulness opposed to frightfulness!' The military authorities certainly recognised the importance of cleanliness. Hot water baths were provided for the troops near the electric light station on the cattle market in Bury. A hot bath, soap and towel cost 2d (60p) and well over 3,000 men used the facilities in June and July. Tin baths were supplied to households who had billeted troops, but these were more often used for coal storage rather than bathing.

Despite the terrifying Zeppelin raids, Bury St Edmunds still didn't really 'get it' that lights would guide the Zeppelins straight to the town at night. There seemed to be a general belief that the previous raid had somehow been an unfortunate oversight and that the bombers were really after the coastal ports or the industrialised northern towns. The Germans appeared, however, to work on the principle of 'if you can see it, bomb it'. Therefore, lighting restrictions were further increased which, if carried out, would make the town invisible from the surrounding countryside. Major Prest, the chief constable of West Suffolk, based in Bury, had been told to inform inhabitants that, under the DORA regulations, the following restrictions would be in force:

1. public lighting was to be reduced to an absolute minimum
2. all lamps to be either extinguished, lowered, obscured or shaded so they could not be seen from above

3. external shop and advertising lights to be extinguished
4. internal shop lights to be reduced and shaded
5. powerful lights on motor or other vehicles were prohibited
6. all lights to be extinguished if an attack was imminent

The Mayor of Bury fully supported the restrictions and issued a serious warning that all offenders would be 'drastically punished'. As summer turned into autumn and the hours of darkness lengthened, the council resolved to whiten the edges of pavements and certain obstructions to reduce mishaps, but there continued to be numerous lighting infringements and flashlights were condemned as 'a disgraceful nuisance'. By November, Oliver's grocers were unable to deliver orders in town after 5pm and some country orders had to be sent by post. Warnings that Zeppelin commanders could see even the small red glow from a cigarette being smoked in the street were generally ignored. Special constables were sworn in to enforce lighting regulations, but they were often resented and abused. Infringements continued, to the extent that, whereas fines for infringement in other towns mainly varied between 10s (£36) and £1 (£72), in Bury St Edmunds fines started at £2 (£144).

In July, the *Bury Free Press* celebrated its diamond jubilee and received numerous accolades. 'May the *Bury Free Press* ... continue to be the mouthpiece of outspoken honest criticism, and comment, and the accurate recorder of passing events.' Although a sense of anti-climax was experienced as the chimes of the Moyse's Hall and St Mary's church clocks were silenced until further notice. The paper raised a smile or two, however, when it ran an advertisement for a Bantam Battalion to be formed and some wit advised that this was for men of smaller stature and not for tiny chickens. Bantam recruits had to be 5ft–5ft 2ins (1.5m–1.55m) and to have a 33-inch (88cm) chest when expanded.

The move was part of the continuous recruitment drive necessary to try and recruit enlisters in sufficient numbers. The Suffolks were suffering heavy losses in France, and on the first anniversary of the war a service was held in the cathedral and prayers were said for the troops. Lord Derby initiated the idea for a national registration scheme under which all adults would have to complete a form stating their name, address, gender, age, marital status, occupation, employer, and number of dependants. The Act ratifying this scheme had been passed, but many suspected it was simply a back door attempt to ascertain the number of males of military age who could be called-up. Sunday 18 August was designated Registration Day. All sections of all forms had to be completed in full on that day and there were penalties for refusing to do so. Occupations and work skills were to be defined and described in detail. The town was divided into thirty-one enumeration districts, and there were forty-six occupation groups for males and thirty for females, each group having sixteen sub-divisions. Particulars of all males aged 16 to 41 were copied onto pink forms. Copies were made of all other forms and registration certificates handed out to each registered person. Copies were also made of forms giving workers' secondary skills. All the information was then entered in the enumerator's book and tabular totals were forwarded to the registrar general. It was a mammoth administrative task that was completed within six weeks. Some pink forms were starred indicating that a man was engaged in either direct war work (like munitions manufacture or driving supply trains) or in an occupation regarded as essential (such as shipbuilding, engineering, farming or forestry, etc). All those men whose pink forms were not starred would be immediately canvassed with a view to persuading them to either enlist immediately or to 'attest' (to be willing to offer military service when called upon to do so). In addition, a big recruiting rally was held in Bury St Edmunds shortly afterwards on 2 October aimed at encouraging Suffolk and Cambridgeshire men to enlist.

There were large advertisements promoting investment in the war loan scheme. Certificates, in multiples of £5 (£360) or vouchers for 5s (£18), 10s (£36) or £1 (£72), could be bought at the post office. David Lloyd George called them 'silver bullets'. These could be cashed in at any time but there was a 4.5 per cent return of 2s 3d (about £8) every six months for each £5 that remained invested.

Thrift was strongly advocated. The Victorians had prided themselves on thrift and economy but this was austerity on a scale that even they had never envisaged. A thrift conference was held in nearby Sudbury and thrift was taught in schools. Economy cookery classes were discussed. The local paper offered weekly hints and recipes.

Suffolk pie could be made with either rabbit or fish depending where in Suffolk one lived. Mushroom pudding and hedgerow cookery were also popular. There would be more natural foods available in a rural area with a comparatively low population density than in the towns, although Bury St Edmunds was still rural enough to enjoy similar advantages. Local sewing groups and work circles for women provided comforts and clothing for the troops for the approaching winter. Bury women undertook house-to-house and street collections in the town for hospital funds as well as caring for the wounded and refugees, and they helped to organise concerts in aid of the Suffolk wool fund for the troops' comforts.

Despite labour shortages, the harvest had got under way, but very few females were employed. Continental countries were happy to use female labour on farms, but not Britain. The government called it stupid. Female workers called it discrimination. Farmers called it prudence, although they rejected as much male labour as female labour on various grounds. Farmers came in for some criticism. 'British farmers do not make good co-operators ... they need to be less isolationist and own way minded', and these were given as reasons for the neglect of egg production and egg marketing. The development of the egg industry had been sadly neglected and, as imported eggs were no longer available, there was an acute short-age of eggs. In addition British farmers were deeply suspicious of the cheaper fertilisers and cattle feeds being used on the Continent. Horses were also in short supply, a problem for local fire brigades as well as on farms.

It was tentatively suggested that farmers should consider farming co-operatives and farming implement co-operatives, which would reduce the need for labour and horses. But many farmers had a somewhat Luddite approach to machinery and, in any case, they simply wanted their sons back from the Front to help.

In November, despite the war and all the pleas for economy, Bury St Edmunds decided to plan lavish celebrations for St Edmund's Day (the 20th). The saint's day in 1914 marked the 700th anniversary of the drawing up of Magna Carta in the abbey at Bury. June 1915 marked the anniversary of the signing of the famous charter and, war or no war, Bury had no intention of letting the occasion go un-remarked. The 700th anniversary would not come again. There was a civic procession to the high altar of the abbey and the placing of a wreath by the mayor. The master of pageantry gave a speech and a benediction to celebrate the anniversary. St Edmund's flag day, held for sailors in the town, raised £165.16s.4d (£11,870). The story of Magna Carta was re-enacted and its implications for the present were emphasised. Laurel wreaths, the symbol of victory, were worn by all

those representing the barons, and the play ended with a short poetic
dedication:

The knights are dust
Their good swords rust
Their souls with the saints
We trust.

The *Bury Free Press* carried a long description of the 'impressive
ceremony and imposing civic procession' and commented that it was
'a fine spectacle ... it was also a powerful lesson in English history
and it conveyed an injunction that we must not forget or disregard'. It
was a statement by the town in defiance of the official discouragement
of 'frivolous celebrations', and it was also a message of defiance to the
enemy.

There was much praise in the town for the Suffolks and Bury
Volunteer Training Corps (VTC). Recruiting pressure was high.
Canvassing for Lord Derby's recruiting scheme intensified and it was
noted that some men were emigrating to escape military call-up.
David Lloyd George and other government ministers had by now
realised that voluntary enlistment was not going to produce sufficient
recruits and that compulsory conscription would be needed to get the
necessary numbers. Recruits from Lord Derby's scheme in Bury were
to receive their training with Bury VTC. In addition, Lord Derby
wanted Red Cross workers to enlist, and there was much discussion
as to whether teachers should enlist as well.

Workers in some starred occupations were being called-up and this
was causing much resentment, especially from farmers complaining
about the lack of skilled ploughmen and harvest helpers. The VTC,
now guarding the railways against possible enemy action in addition
to their other duties, held a church parade in Barningham, a village
some 13 miles from Bury St Edmunds, and the rector of Barningham
said in his address that 'behind a heroic army and navy we must have
a heroic nation'.

The *Bury Free Press* carried regular pages of war news and casualties, as well as a series of cartoons to try and lighten the general
gloom. One showed the kaiser with King Sweyn, an eleventh-century
Danish king who led an invasion of England in 1013 and was
crowned King of England on Christmas Day that year. Doubtless the
inference was that the kaiser, a supposedly cultured twentieth-century
European military leader, was reduced to asking Sweyn, a rough and

ready eleventh-century Viking, for advice on how to invade and subdue Britain.

The town determined to try and remain upbeat for Christmas and the whole front page and page 2 of the local paper for 11 December were full of advertisements and features on where to purchase Christmas gifts and food. Oranges were provided for patients at the Isolation Hospital and Christmas entertainments for the troops were provided for soldiers in the town. The Athenaeum Hall had also been let to the YMCA as a recreation room over the Christmas period. The Athenaeum choir performed *Hiawatha* (by Samuel Coleridge).

There was a general decline in the number of cards, letters and telegrams this year, but there was an increase in cables abroad and parcels. Parcels for those at the Front could contain whisky, plum pudding, Christmas cake, chocolate and any other little treats that were not perishable. Drapers announced they would close on Christmas Eve until the following Wednesday, and many other shops followed suit. Mistletoe was picked from oak, apple and chestnut trees and holly was cut from hedges to decorate houses, hospital wards and public halls. The vicar of St James provided a large Christmas tree for 600 children whose fathers and brothers were away serving at the Front. However, noticeable numbers of loved ones were missing from the celebrations which, although enjoyable, were rather quiet, and it was fervently hoped that this Christmas would be the last Christmas of the war.

CHAPTER 3

1916

As the New Year dawned the hope of most folk was victory, peace, prosperity and, of course, to have their loved ones home safe. An intercession service for the war and those involved in it was held on the first Sunday of the year in St Mary's Church.

The *Bury Free Press* began the year with a series of questions for the farming community. Why had they depended on German potash for fertiliser when potash could be made in Britain from burning kelp? The women could do it as they did in the tiny Isles of Scilly off the Cornish coast. There was a shortage of animal feeding stuffs, so why was Britain still exporting barley, barley meal, malt and 'milling offals', which could be used for this purpose? Although the sugar-beet campaign was progressing, there was still much debate as to whether Britain could or should produce its own sugar. There was little question about 'could', but 'should' was another matter. The egg industry was not receiving either the attention or the input it required despite the best efforts of Great Eastern Railway, who were running a special egg industry promotion train around East Anglia.

Prevarication now seemed to be a keyword within the farming industry, whose aims and objectives centred around the repatriation of farmers' sons from the Front. The government was fast losing patience with the industry as a whole, and it was considering bringing in legislation to force farmers to accept female workers and to grow whatever was required. There was already a plan in the borough of Bury St Edmunds to revive the village industry of medicinal herbs, as had happened on the continent. Herb farming was something that women could and would do. Besides, they would also willingly help out as farm labourers, despite certain derogatory comments on the subject made by a man from Cornard, a village a few miles from Bury. 'Ha!' he sneered. 'They could not get a woman to work in the house in this village, let alone on a farm!'

The lighting restrictions were still causing considerable controversy, being condemned as 'now overdone and a great inconvenience'. The streets remained darkened and car headlights were severely curtailed. Accidents were common and attacks on lone women increased. Flashlights were considered useful if properly utilised, but 'thoughtless and reckless youth is responsible for wild and indiscriminate flashing which is irritating and dangerous'. However, one citizen of Bury refused to let the problems get him down. 'Darkness,' he wrote, 'has beauty and advantage despite bumping into lamp posts.'

The burning question, meanwhile, was compulsory conscription. It had become evident by the summer of 1915 that voluntary enlistment was not going to produce sufficient numbers for the armed forces, and conscription was being seriously debated. The minister for education, Arthur Henderson, warned that there would be severe problems enforcing compulsory conscription because 40 per cent of men still did not have the vote, and it would cause enormous resentment if they were forced to fight, by a parliament they had not elected, for a country in whose government they could play no part. Furthermore, casualties were so high there was a big risk that many would not return. David Lloyd George was a realist, however. After the disaster of Gallipoli and the Dardanelles, there were simply not enough men left to fight on all fronts and he knew that compulsory conscription, difficult though it might be, was all that would save Britain from annihilation.

In January 1916, the Military Service Bill was passed. All single men and childless widowers between the ages of 18 and 41 now had three choices:

1. to enlist immediately
2. to attest at once under the Derby Scheme and join the army or navy
3. to be automatically assumed to have enlisted on 2 March.

There was a huge outcry. Up to this point married men had enlisted in greater numbers than unmarried men and had complained that single men were not doing their share. Now single men claimed unfair discrimination. Consequently, in May the Bill was extended to cover married men and, from April, the upper age limit was raised to 50–56 as need arose. However, as Henderson had warned, compulsion proved a step too far. By July, 93,000 (30 per cent of those so far called-up) were guilty of a 'no show'. Military service tribunals were set up in towns and cities across the country so that men could appeal on grounds of:

- war work or reserved occupations
- hardship
- medically unfit
- conscientious objection

Reserved or exempted occupations included:

- agricultural work
- forestry
- shipbuilding
- munitions manufacture
- coal mining
- iron and steel workers
- doctors
- clergymen

Most tribunals gave few exemptions for other jobs, and those that were granted were often only temporary. Bury St Edmunds made several exemptions on work grounds and indispensability, however. Bury folk accepted important war work or a good medical reason as reasonable grounds for exemption, but everyone was suffering hardship and they had no time at all for conscientious objectors. These were nick-named 'slackers', and statements were made in the local paper such as 'conscience doth make cowards of us all' and 'some wars just have to be fought'.

At the same time a Derby-style scheme had been canvassing and recruiting females for agricultural work. There was no shortage of volunteers. The main problem was the prejudice of the farmers. The Marchioness of Bristol undertook the organisation of the West Suffolk branch of Women for Agricultural Service. A registrar was appointed for groups of parishes, and meetings arranged. Parish registrars were to make appeals to women within their parishes who were eligible for agricultural work and they would keep a register of female workers for local farms, as well as women willing to train and to work away from home. Their hardest task would be to persuade farmers who were short of labour to employ women. Many farmers were still holding out for repatriation of their sons for ploughing and the harvest, but it was not practical or financially viable to keep doing this and the government was determined to make farmers accept the use of female labour.

In West Suffolk, the Marchioness's scheme had 1,400 women registered and ready to work on the land. By March, farmers in Norfolk had accepted female workers on their land and had been impressed with both the quality and quantity of their work. The women worked from 8.00am–4.00pm for 2/- (just over £6) per day. The pressure was now on for West Suffolk, including Bury St Edmunds, to follow suit. Female milkers were employed but were not to be paid more than £1 (£60) a week. Women were also good at rearing calves or acting as shepherds, and they were encouraged to cultivate allotments as well.

There was a noticeable increase in war weddings in Bury, as there was everywhere else, and 'pretty khaki weddings' became a weekly event dutifully reported in the local paper. Many couples just wanted to snatch whatever time they could have together, although for some there was a 'last chance saloon' feel about it. Weddings were generally a simpler affair a hundred years ago, with far more emphasis on the religious aspect and less on expensive trimmings and accessories. Wealthier girls could afford a white dress but for most, the wedding outfit was a dress or two-piece, which could be worn on several future occasions, and a small bunch of wild flowers. There was little time and less money for honeymoons.

As well as celebrating numbers of local weddings, Bury also determined to mark the tercentenary of Shakespeare's death in 1616, especially for schoolchildren, and, as a prelude, the Theatre Royal staged *A Midsummer Night's Dream* to raise funds for the VTC.

Certified female teachers and pupil teachers were now replacing male teachers serving in the forces. There had been a drop in the numbers of children attending school and there was talk of reducing staff still further to economise on the salary bill. Further economy measures were the suspension of school medical inspections, and 'dog nuisances' were allowed to become a problem. On the plus side, agricultural education was now taught in schools, and elementary schools were insured against aircraft risk.

On a different and more controversial note, the *Bury Free Press* was alarmed by talk of disbanding the Suffolk foxhounds. 'Fox hunting is one of the best and oldest British sports,' the paper stated, 'and it might be difficult to re-establish it.'

April arrived amid heavy snow and howling gales, which caused a lot of damage in East Anglia. Thousands of trees were blown down and drainage work was damaged. In Bury, the Abbey Gardens lost a lime tree that was nearly a century old, and there was some damage to houses as well as several accidents and injuries. Even worse than that, however, was the second Zeppelin raid on the town, which began just before midnight on 31 March and continued into the early hours of 1 April. Although on this occasion the town was darkened, the Zeppelin airship, L16, commanded by Werner Petersen, left a swathe of death and destruction in 'a storm of bombs'. The first bombs fell near Northgate Railway Station, and Eastgate Railway Station was also hit. Properties in Mill Road, Chalk Road, Raingate Street and Prussia Lane were damaged. Four people, including a mother and her two young children, died in Mill Road, two men died in Raingate Street near the King of Prussia pub, and one soldier from the Cambridgeshire Regiment died on Chalk Road. In total, seven people were killed, five people were injured and thirty-seven houses damaged. A horse, a dog and a cat were also killed. Bury St Edmunds was deeply shocked. Despite precautions and all the lighting restrictions, this attack had been far worse than the previous one, which had taken place on a clear moonlit night with the town clearly visible.

The funerals of the dead were a solemn but impressive public affair, with people lining the streets, the line of black hearses unbearably sad, the victims deeply mourned. The whole episode induced in Bury what would probably be described as a kind of collective post-traumatic stress reaction.

The town became obsessed with lighting restrictions and blackouts and measures to deal with aerial attacks, and remained so, long after the main danger from Zeppelin attacks had faded and the government had relaxed restrictions. Even when peace was finally declared in 1918, the town was cautious about fully displaying its lights again.

Zeppelins kept up their attacks on East Anglia throughout April until, on Easter Monday at the end of April, they were repulsed by anti-aircraft guns, followed by a naval battle off Lowestoft that was won by the Royal Navy. The total casualties from this aerial battle over the Suffolk coast was a dead bullock and 'one roasted turkey'. Rather than being reassured by the successful use of anti-aircraft guns, Bury came close to a state of panic. They worried about the blue air-raid lamps providing inadequate warning of raids and about the time it would take to extinguish all lights in case of attack. They worried about being told not to go to the shelters until the Zeppelins actually arrived. Street patrols at night, watching for Zeppelins, were instigated, although they caused a lot of anxiety and 'had something of the vigilante about them'. Knowing the chief constable disapproved of private patrols for this purpose, the mayor tried to still people's fears in a manner that was a cross between a stern headmaster and a strict sergeant major. He voiced his disapproval of 'deprecating exhibitions of cowardice and panic which are unEnglish' and despised 'those who have developed into "blancmanges" through air fright'. In the mayor's opinion the existing precautions against Zeppelin air-raids were quite adequate. Many in the town clearly thought otherwise. It is hard to understand exactly how terrified the townspeople felt but it must be remembered that this was the first time in history aerial warfare had been used. Until this point folk had believed that if they were in their own country, and it was not under enemy occupation, they were safe. This was no longer the case and it never would be again.

A service was held for serving soldiers in the cathedral on Good Friday, but Easter was generally a subdued affair. Ignoring the view that, in general, any festivities were regarded as frivolous, Bury St Edmunds held tercentenary celebrations for Shakespeare on 23 April, the actual date of his death. Special badges were issued to local students and a celebration was held at the West Suffolk County School in Bury with 'effective dramatic representation'. There was an inspiring address by the headmaster, who alluded fulsomely to Shakespeare, his works and his talent, which could 'convert certain plays into finest gold'.

Three hundred years away from Shakespeare, the military tribunals in Bury were working hard, almost overwhelmed by the many appeals for exemption from military call-up, mostly from farmers for their sons and farmhands. The farmers were not giving up without a fight and continued to insist that they needed to work their land jointly with their sons. Many were totally resistant to female labour, despite the best efforts of the Marchioness of Bristol. Horses were standing idle, the farmers maintained, because females could not drive a cart or do the corn threshing, nor were there any men to look after the livestock. The tribunals were unimpressed, especially now having plenty of evidence to the contrary. Besides, they knew the so-called lack of manpower was not the real reason. There were plenty of male prisoners-of-war, Irish labourers and boy scouts available. It had become a battle of wills. On the one hand, the farmers were determined to force the government to repatriate their sons. On the other hand, the government had no intention of doing so and every intention of forcing the farmers to accept the labour that was available. The bishops of Norwich, Oxford and Lincoln spoke out darkly about the use of child labour, criticising a return to the bad old days. The government retorted that the prisoners-of-war and Irish labourers were grown men and that many of the boy scouts were over 14 years old, while female workers were at least 17. The Bury tribunals were also unimpressed by appeals from builders, blacksmiths, millers, grocery assistants, fish fryers and foresters' secretaries. One miller pleaded that he could not run a steam-mill and a wind-mill without assistance. However, the steam-mill could do the work of both, although not so cheaply, so the miller's assistant's appeal was refused, and the miller's lost profits were gauged to be his contribution to the war effort.

In order to conserve fuel, Germany and Austria introduced daylight saving time in April 1916. The clocks were put forward one hour in order to maximise the usage of natural daylight. Allied and neutral countries rapidly followed suit, with British daylight saving time being introduced for the first time on 21st May 1916. Some farmers didn't quite understand the idea at first, and assumed their milking staff would now have to rise at 3.00am as this was the new 4.00am. They confused both themselves and everyone else, causing not a little amusement along the way. On the whole, daylight saving time was well received despite a few grumbles about children going to bed later and becoming over-tired as a result. The principle was welcomed, however, and 100 years later daylight saving time is still part of the British summer.

Three days later, on 24 May, Bury St Edmunds, still ignoring the national disinclination for any festivities, celebrated Empire Day for the first time. 'Scarred relics of the great historic past' were on exhibition. There was an impressive pageant and a spectacular display on Angel Hill, and a Red Cross flag day was held on the same day, which raised £287 (£17,380) for the benefit of sailors. The authorities hoped that shows of patriotism and the flag would make deep impressions on local, younger minds. There was concern about increasing juvenile crime in the area. The causes were considered to be absentee fathers and working mothers, a lack of discipline and respect, and watching too many unsuitable films in the cinema. Little has changed. Empire Day proved a success with the only criticism levelled at random parking of cars, 'which had not been allowed in the days of the horse and cart'.

Along with the rest of the country, the people of Bury were now in for a fresh shock. Lord Kitchener, the commander-in-chief of the army, whose image and outstretched pointing hand appeared on recruiting posters with the slogan 'Your country needs you', was drowned on 5 June on his way to attend negotiations in Russia. His ship, HMS *Hampshire*, struck a German mine and sank just west of the Orkney Islands. Over 600 men on board died with him and the sinking was declared a national tragedy. Services of remembrance were held in local churches all over the country and there was a genuine feeling of loss. Lord Kitchener was succeeded by General Sir Douglas Haig, who would mastermind the Battle of the Somme.

Bury Red Cross followed their successful flag day in May with a mammoth sale of 'livestock' and 'deadstock' at the cattle market ground. The livestock included sheep, bullocks, calves, pigs, poultry, horses and donkeys while the deadstock consisted of eggs, butter, grain, meal, hardware, etc. Black-faced Suffolk sheep were 'noted prize-winners and ideal for butchers'. It raised nearly £4,000 (£242,000). Although farmers had donated quite generously to the Red Cross sale, the shortage of agricultural labour was becoming a matter of urgency. Two hundred and fifty thousand agricultural men had been called to the colours so far, and cows were being slaughtered due to a lack of male workers to milk them. Farmers now insisted that the cows didn't like female milkers, thereby completely ignoring the centuries-old tradition of English milkmaids and the more prosaic fact that cows simply wanted the pressure on their udders relieved by milking and didn't much care who did it. Meanwhile, the government was fast losing patience and condemned farmers as 'short sighted, narrow minded and prejudiced' for their refusal to accept prisoners-of-war, female workers, Irish labourers and older men on their farms. The farmers wanted their sons and cheap schoolboy labour. To try and help, the Whitsunday school holidays were postponed and an extra week given at harvest-time so that the children could help out, but it was not enough and teachers grumbled about the lack of notice given for re-arranging the school holidays.

Until the summer of 1916, Bury St Edmunds, despite the Zeppelin attacks, had not suffered as badly as some towns and cities, especially those in the north of England in areas of heavy population density.

Bury was a rural market town set among thousands of acres of fertile countryside whose main industry was farming and farming products. There was no heavy industry, no empty mills and manufactories, no specialist or luxury services, the lack of which would greatly affect the economic life of the town or, more importantly, the food supply. Everyone had friends or family in the countryside and fresh food-stuffs could always be found. Elsewhere the effects of the Germans blockading British coasts and sinking as many merchant ships as they could to try and starve the country into submission were being felt in varying degrees, but in Bury little was noticed other than a short-age of sugar. There had been a few bankruptcies in the town, mainly caused by small businesses collapsing, usually due to owners, managers and staff being called-up. They were casualties of war but not on a large scale. There was, however, one industry of crucial importance to the war that was so secret that many in Bury did not even know of it, although it changed the face and course of the war.

The small Suffolk village of Elveden lies 10 miles to the north of Bury St Edmunds. Elveden Hall had been the home of Duleep Singh, the last Maharaja of the Punjab, and the place where Prince Freddie spent his boyhood. Duleep Singh lies buried with his wife Bamba in the churchyard at Elveden. The grounds of the hall were extensive and it was here that the first armoured tanks were tried and tested and men were trained to operate them. The idea of a 'land battleship' had been discussed for some time as a way of breaking the deadlock on the Western Front. Inspired by the use of armoured trains on the South African veldt during the Boer War, an officer from the Royal Engineers, Lieutenant Colonel E.D. Swinton, developed the idea of armoured motor vehicles running on caterpillar tracks to break through the German lines of defence. The first prototype, Little Willie, derisively named after the kaiser, was built by Fosters of Lincoln late in 1915. Early in 1916, its successor, known as either Big Willie or Mother, was built and became the model for Mark One tanks used during the latter part of the Great War. These tanks were further refined into 'male' and 'female'. 'Male' tanks were heavily armed for use against bunkers and enemy artillery, while the 'female' tanks only carried machine-guns and were used primarily against trenches and infantry. Full scale production amid great secrecy began in February 1916, and the tanks were transported from Lincoln to Elveden under cover labelled as freight bound for Russia. Such was

Land Battleship – Battle of the Somme 1916.

the secrecy involved that even those manufacturing the machines were not told their true purpose, simply that they were mobile water tanks. Workers took to referring to them simply as tanks, which was how 'landships' acquired their colloquial name. Once at Elveden the tanks were painted in a mixture of camouflage colours including pink, grey, green and brown blotches. Swinton then recreated an imitation battlefield of 25 square miles (about 44 square km) within the grounds of Elveden Hall in order to fully test the machines and train their operators. North Stow Farm lay well within the perimeter and was used as a shooting target. Everyone connected with any aspect of the tank project was sworn to maintain complete secrecy and the penalty for doing otherwise was to be accused of treason, a crime that carried the death penalty. Even today Elveden is fairly remote and scarcely populated. In 1916 it was the ideal setting for such a venture. Roger Pugh has written an excellent book, *The Most Secret Place on Earth*, on the complete history of tank testing and training at Elveden during the Great War. The most secret place it proved to be, for the Germans had absolutely no idea of what was happening and were completely taken by surprise when tanks first appeared on the battlefields of the Somme in September 1916 to replace the hapless Allied infantrymen who had previously been ordered to run unprotected into sub-machine-gunfire. These 'weird and wonderful engines of destruction' were said to have left the Germans 'bewildered and terrified'.

The Battle of the Somme, which began on 1 July 1916, was a major turning point in the Great War and even Bury could not escape its consequences. David Lloyd George had been against the battle from the start, saying it would be a great disaster and a complete waste of manpower and resources that the country could ill afford. General Sir Douglas Haig told him, in effect, not to be so silly. Lloyd George was not a military man, said Haig. He couldn't possibly understand the principles of good battle strategy. The Battle of the Somme would be a resounding one-day success and would completely rout the Germans. Haig was so confident of his predictions that he arranged for cameras to film the battle as it happened. In the event, the Battle of the Somme lasted over four months and was one of the biggest military disasters in history. There were well over a million casualties and at least 300,000 men died. The battle virtually wiped out a whole battalion of the Suffolk Regiment. Mr H. Goodfellow of Bury lost three of his four sons. 'The great advance at Ypres going well' but despite the cheerful war propaganda, the glory and patriotism of war had suddenly turned into a massive and unbelievably bloody carnage on the muddy battlefields of France. It stunned everyone.

Tank in use on the Western Front, November 1916.

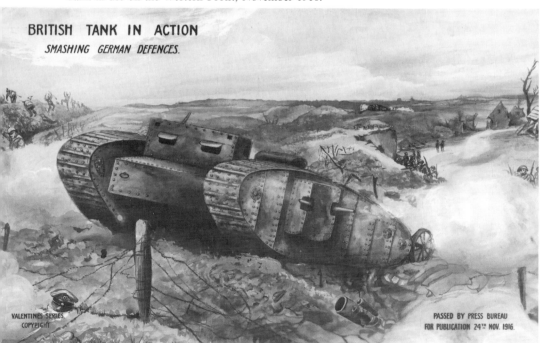

BRITISH TANK IN ACTION
SMASHING GERMAN DEFENCES.

VALENTINES SERIES
COPYRIGHT

PASSED BY PRESS BUREAU
FOR PUBLICATION 24TH NOV. 1916.

British tank capturing German soldiers, c.1917.

Intercession services were held to mark the third anniversary of war in Bury churches, and then, in early August, Zeppelin airships again invaded East Anglia over the period of a week. Great aerial fleets appeared in the skies over Suffolk. Bury folk huddled together in darkened places and prayed desperately that the town would not be hit for a third time. Large numbers of bombs were dropped but they did not cause as much devastation as on previous occasions. Meadows and ditches were bombed. Some horses were killed and injured. Otherwise there was not much real damage, despite a fleet of twelve Zeppelins attacking coastal towns. The towns attacked were not named and there was a general news blackout. The papers simply referred to 'German air frightfulness abroad again'. Bury St Edmunds, to its great relief, was not attacked this time as darkness and mist hampered the vision of the airships over inland towns and villages. On the coast two airships were brought down by anti-aircraft guns. The fight-back was beginning in earnest. A week later the Zeppelins returned to the east coast, but further north this time. In the north-east, six people and a horse were killed, seventeen people were injured and a number of houses were burned. Bury folk were horrified and sympathetic, but also relieved that it was not them suffering again. The Zeppelin raids on East Anglia continued for the rest of August but with minimal damage and no casualties. Anti-aircraft gun defences were becoming more efficient, which resulted in much greater caution on the part of the Zeppelin commanders. In early September, tentative peace proposals were put forward by the Germans but were rejected by the Allies, who wanted retribution not 'a patched up peace'. A week later, thirteen Zeppelins attempted an invasion, which resulted in disappointment for the Germans. Disturbed cattle gave warning of the approaching airships so there were few casualties and only slight damage. An officer of the Royal Flying Corps brought down one of the Zeppelins, for which the king subsequently awarded him the Victoria Cross. The remaining airships were driven from London and heavily shelled. As they flew over East Anglia on their way home they dropped many bombs but succeeded only in hitting fields and heathland and destroying a turnip crop. Those who heard them described a sinister drumming noise and the 'eerie chug chug of engines' as they passed overhead but the raiders were baffled by the absolute darkness and had no idea where they were dropping their bombs.

Despite the Zeppelin raids and the terror of Bury folk there were still problems with obscuring lights and still great resentment of the special constables who attempted to enforce the lighting restrictions as well as the regulation to avoid talking in the streets in groups. A number of folk in Risbygate Street showed their defiance by talking, lighting cigarettes and smoking in the street. Their foolhardiness could be both seen and heard from above, but the specials persevered in the face of this hostility and ensured that the town was in complete darkness and silence during Zeppelin raids, although they received scant thanks.

On the Home Front, Bury now began to really feel the effects of the war. As a result of unscrupulous profiteering and shortages the government had begun to regulate sugar supplies and were taking control of the wheat supply as well to stabilise prices. There were grumbles that austerity was preventing essential road repairs from being carried out, especially on Hospital Road, amid numerous complaints of reckless cyclists dashing about town on the wrong side of the road without lights. Local labour shortages were adversely affecting the Abbey Gardens. Thefts of flowers and general pilfering had been reported. The Rechabites (an organisation of teetotallers) were trying to prevent all sales of alcohol during the course of the war. The reason, they insisted, was that the temptation of drink should be removed from the troops. Waste paper collection had been advocated and a ton was collected in Bury by the girl guides. Clothes, hats, boots and tobacco were now all subject to stringent economies. Some dairymen were selling milk 'not of the nature, substance or quality demanded'. Overdue rates accounts were being chased in several parishes. Some were also defaulting on payments to the Board of Guardians for the workhouse, although there was a general decrease in vagrancy, but as much as £1,200 (over £72,000) remained in outstanding contributions. Bury Gas Company managed to break even, although the electricity company was struggling. The prisoner-of-war funds committee members were doing good work and had raised £500 (over £30,000) for food and comfort parcels to be sent to Bury men and the Suffolks who were being held prisoner by the Germans. Another committee was appointed to organise and oversee storage of soldiers' furniture. Soldiers' and sailors' welfare organisations were kept busy. The August bank holiday was abolished and Hardwick Fête abandoned.

Meanwhile, the local military tribunals were still working full-time hearing appeals and the farmers were still causing problems. The harvest prospects looked set fair, but the authorities still found themselves having to repatriate soldiers who were farmers' sons to help out. Lloyd George was furious and vowed, when he became prime minister in December, that the government would do whatever it took to force the farmers to fall in line.

Towards the end of September, Bury traders met to discuss the possibility of early closing and the difficulties this might cause. Those in favour said it would save on gas, lighting, electricity and coal. Shop assistants would be allowed three-quarters of an hour for tea if shops closed at 6.00pm, and it would also enable them to get home earlier, which would be advantageous on dark nights in dark streets. Some believed that 6.00pm closing was 'absolutely ridiculous', especially for the grocery trades, but admitted that the darkened streets and the air-raid emergencies were major problems. There was also the question of lower profits. Finally it was agreed that shops would shut by 6.00pm Monday–Wednesday, 7.00pm on Friday, and 8.00pm on Saturday. Thursday was designated half-day closing when shops would shut at 1.00pm. The clocks reverted from BST to GMT at 3.00am on Sunday 1st October, going back to 2.00am, and folk got an extra hour in bed. Most traders respected the earlier closing hours but there were a few mavericks, notably in the sweets and tobacco trades. The *Bury Free Press* expressed hope that the public would show their disapproval by ostracising shops that did not adhere to the new opening hours. The paper also hoped that local publicans might follow suit and that clergy 'wedded to evening service' would set an example by altering the times of their services. The cathedral had already done so, but other churches had yet to follow their example.

The borough council had a difficult meeting that October. The rule of 'keep to the right' in darkened streets, using the whitened edges of the pavements as a guide, was being broken with monotonous regularity and attendant injuries, often caused by folk falling over drunks in the street. It was also suggested that women should wear white hats or headscarves at night. The mayor complained angrily in council chambers about the use of bright lights. Shopkeepers were fined and he hoped that guilty motorists would be booked for the offence. Meanwhile, the electricity company was having problems with the supply, which was prone to interruption and causing the air-raid warning lights to malfunction. After the mayor had finished complaining about lighting restriction infringements, there was a shouting match over the Risbygate sewers, which were overflowing. The sewer levels were not intended to rise more than 4 inches (10cm) with excess rainwater, but this had happened despite some insistence to the contrary and it was alleged that the water could reach knee-deep. Virtually all maintenance work had ceased as a result of the war. However, it was obvious that the sewage overflow situation in Risbygate would have to be resolved and tempers flared with some saying that knee-deep water was an exaggeration and that the situation wasn't actually that bad.

Rates now exceeded 8/- (£24) in the £1 (£60), but still there was little money available for emergency maintenance work. Teachers had been granted a war bonus to help with the high and still rising cost of living, and this had increased outgoings under the education budget.

In November, Guy Fawkes celebrations were banned, as they had been since 1914, which resulted in much glumness among the children. The post office now closed every afternoon throughout the week, causing both concern and inconvenience. It was also decided that Sunday closing of shops should now be observed according to an Act passed in the time of Charles II and that street traders should be banned on the Sabbath. A number of folk thought that the pubs should be included in Sunday closing as well. Bury was placed out of bounds after 5.00pm anyway by the military authorities. Traffic obstruction on Wednesday market days was causing problems due to parked cars, and so parking restrictions were brought into force. Newspaper boys were told to cease shouting their wares and knocking on doors. Vandalism was reported in the park and the public toilets, emphasising the need for more discipline within the town. There was a number of disturbances at dances held in the town hall with the result that town hall lets ceased at 10.00pm. All charities and collectors now had to submit applications to the Registered Charities Board due to new regulations passed to counteract bogus charities and collections. Bury also decided that it wanted to follow London's lead and organise 'a systematic crusade against Germanism' after the war was over. The British Empire Women's League led the way, stating its aims of 'keeping out Germans, German trade and German ways' because the German character had been found to be 'disgusting, brutal and treacherous'. Strong words, but the local paper had often referred to Germans as 'the baby killers' after Zeppelin raids. War casualty lists seemed endless. All in all, November was a grim month and an unpromising advent to Christmas.

Bury found itself looking forward to a somewhat low-key Christmas. The government was running out of various essential supplies and an appeal was made in the town for spare razors to be sent out to the troops. Soldiers in Egypt appealed for mouth organs and accordions 'to relieve the monotony of desert life'. Parcels of food, comforts and tobacco were posted by local families to their loved ones overseas. Despite the problems, however, a smoking concert was held for the military at the Theatre Royal and a cinema licence was granted to the Athenaeum Hall to show films to soldiers. The VTC headquarters on Crown Street was also made available for all comfort for the troops. Proceeds from a Friday matinee showing of the Battle of the Somme in the town were donated to Suffolk prisoner-of-war funds. Fuel shortages were becoming acute, and constant pleas were made for economy. Housewives were asked to cook 'one pot' meals to save on fuel. Gas and electric lights were now lowered as intimation of air-raid warnings and then turned off three minutes later. If this occurred at night the gas would remain turned off until the following morning. Under increased lighting restrictions the town hall could not be let in the evenings during the first and last quarters of the moon.

Train journeys were severely curtailed over the Christmas and New Year periods and fares increased by 50 per cent. Food shortages were becoming a critical problem, even in rural areas like Suffolk. Imports were now severely restricted, especially of dried and tinned fruit, and pork supplies were threatened by the slaughter of young pigs owing to high feeding costs. For those going out to dinner, the 'fashionable dining time' moved from 8.30pm back to 6.30pm to accommodate food and fuel economy and, in summer, daylight saving hours. Someone discovered that an Act of Edward III (1327–1377) was still on the statute books and advocated no dining in the evenings. For the rest of the time only two-course meals were to be served with three courses allowed on great occasions. The recommendations of this long dead king were, in fact, already being followed to some extent. Menus were fixed and no more than three courses could be served in public places between 6.00pm and 9.30pm. The sole exception was Christmas Day, when a three course meal could be served at 12.30pm. At other times only two courses were allowed. A helpful guide in the form of the Regulation of Meals Order was issued in mid-December for those in doubt:

soup = half a course
fish/joint = a full course
puddings/celery and cheese = a full course
fruit = half a course
bacon and eggs = two courses

Cheese and bread were not reckoned to be a course. An official meatless days order was issued as well, although a medieval king might have had difficulty in accepting that limitation. However, fish was not regarded as meat so restaurants could serve soup with a fish main course and perhaps a small dessert. Army officers were also given strict limits as to how much they could spend on each meal. Despite all the problems, however, E.E. Westgate grocers in Bury could still offer haricot beans and rice from Japan and Rangoon, lentils from Egypt, blue peas from Japan, and rolled oats from Canada, as well as semolina, tapioca, macaroni and pearl barley. English kiln-dried split peas were also popular. The council was con-sidering suggestions that parks and flower gardens should be turned into allotments to grow food, and they initiated a move to cultivate wasteland and 'hidden plots' in Bury. The council also realised that it would need to ascertain quantities of available seed potatoes for the town and some of the surrounding villages.

There were general Christmas greetings to Bury folk from the mayor and from the king and queen. Despite the disasters of 1916, it was felt that 1917 might be a brighter and better year. Many took heart from the words of Oliver Cromwell. In 1644 he had admitted that military mistakes were made during the course of the Civil War, but that they should be overlooked for the main cause and had urged 'a more rigorous prosecution of the war to avoid a dishonourable peace'. To the people of Bury St Edmunds that summed up an admirable resolution for the new year of 1917.

CHAPTER 4

1917

❧

Intercession Sunday services had been held on New Year's Eve but the first issue of the *Bury Free Press* for 1917 carried a good deal of war news that was not cheerful and the by now ubiquitous long lists of casualties. There were also details of local military awards, which were uplifting for townsfolk, and outcomes of the military tribunals, which were not usually welcome. Fellgets' New Year message was upbeat: 'Victory, Peace & Prosperity', their greeting to 1917. Pretty's held a great stock clearance sale of clothes and household linens, although many did not have much money. Some of the local country houses were advertising for servants, which perhaps emphasised their remoteness from what was actually going on. There was a shortage of domestic labour, as in other professions, due to enlistment, compulsory or otherwise, the acute need for workers in the war industries, especially munitions, and the simple fact that almost any other job paid better wages, an absolute necessity with the rapidly rising costs of living. Some newspapers in neighbouring counties were actually promoting the idea of fewer servants as an economy measure, which also freed up people for the war effort. Following a report that darkened-street accidents were killing hundreds more than Zeppelins, and encouraged by supposed street-light concessions being made in London, Bury made fresh pleas for more street lighting, asking for forty-two instead of the current thirty lights allowed. None was sanctioned, however, and the town was also told it could not have any more blue air-raid warning lamps either, on grounds of health and safety, despite a police recommendation of one for the post office.

Suffolk was increasing food and vegetable production in gardens. Potatoes and onions were in demand and swedes were being promoted as 'tasty vegetables'. In addition, cultivation of wasteland to grow vegetables was encouraged. It was reasoned that if individuals could grow various crops of vegetables, this would allow the farmers to concentrate on wheat, oats and barley, as well as potatoes, with some mangolds for animal fodder. School gardens would also play a part, with pupils taught to grow their own food by tending crops grown by the school, and potatoes were to be cultivated in the Abbey Gardens. The importance of soil types was stressed when deciding what type of crops to grow as some would not take in certain soils. Woolpit School Gardens, a few miles from Bury St Edmunds, had six plots of 1.5 square poles each. A pole is a unit of length equal to 5.5 yards (5.03 metres) for growing food. Vegetables were grown in four plots and a six-year model rotation of crops was practised:

- round onions and spring onions
- peas, intercropped by lettuce and succeeded with turnips
- beet, carrots, parsnips (no manure used)
- autumn onions, turnips and French beans
- early cabbage followed by Brussels sprouts (manured twice)
- potatoes (no manure used)

Another plot was used for propagating fruit trees and growing fruit while the last plot was used for seed beds and general purposes.

A meeting was held at Bury Town Hall about the production of vegetable crops as part of a national move towards home food production, which was becoming vitally important. Potatoes were the chief crop but others, such as onions, carrots, parsnips, swedes, celery, peas, beans, lettuce, tomatoes and cucumber, were to be grown. West Suffolk farmers protested volubly to West Suffolk Agricultural Committee in Bury St Edmunds that farms were being denuded of labour. Everywhere was being denuded of labour was the short and sharp reply, so the plan was that farmers should grow grain, potatoes and animal fodder, and keep dairy herds for meat, milk, cheese and butter, while individuals would grow vegetables and keep chickens and hopefully a pig where facilities allowed. There were lots of new cheap poultry foods on the market, but most free-range hens were quite capable of scratching a decent living on their own, perhaps topped up with occasional household scraps. Applications were invited from those who wanted allotments, while many utilised their own gardens. In the matter of potato cultivation, there would be some overlapping with the Allotments Scheme. Farmers grumbled that understaffing might mean they were planting corn that might not be harvested, but no one paid much attention. The West Suffolk Agricultural Committee vowed to take whatever action was necessary under the Cultivation of Land Order to try and ensure a sufficient supply of food could be home-grown and successfully harvested. A total of seventy-five German prisoners-of-war were offered to work on the land, although thirty-five guards were needed to oversee them and prevent any escape attempts, so this posed an accommodation problem.

Returning troops, wounded or simply on leave, were offered all comforts at the VTC headquarters on Crown Street and the YMCA also helped out. Part of the Guildhall was given over to facilities for wounded soldiers and they were also entertained with concerts, followed by tea at the Athenaeum. The Athenaeum was planning to open a cinema, despite difficulties in obtaining plush 'tip-up' chairs. *The Golden Lotus* was scheduled to be shown on 15 January, followed by *Under the Red Rose* on 18 January. However, these laudable intentions were rather put in the shade when the Empire Cinema in the town announced a showing of *The Tanks* in February.

The Isolation Hospital and Thingoe RDC collaborated on the destruction of rats plaguing the hospital to stop their spread in the town. Rats were a big problem during the Great War and a threat to both food stocks and health.

There was still a drive, especially in the rural areas of West Suffolk, to encourage the purchase of war savings bonds and certificates, which gave a good percentage return, and to invest in war loans. While 'men, munitions and money' were needed, equally important were 'the silver bullets which will decide the war', according to David Lloyd George. The Feoffment Schools in Bury set a fine example by buying war certificates to the value of £118 (just under £6,000) and Bury St Edmunds Town Council contributed £5,000 (£250,200). Appeals were also made to farmers, engineers, builders and smiths, etc, to collect all their scrap metal for use in the production of munitions. There were seventy war savings associations in Bury St Edmunds and its district, a high number given the relatively low population, and large sums were invested in the war certificates.

A move had begun nationally to abolish the grand jury system. This term is more reminiscent of the US, which still retains a grand jury system. The grand jury consisted of between twelve and twenty-three people and had rather different powers. Charges would be put to them, they would only examine prosecution witnesses, and they would then decide if there were sufficient grounds to put an accused person on trial. Grand juries had ceased functioning in the UK by 1933 and were completely abolished in 1948, but they were suspended for the duration of the Great War. Most of their work is now done by the Crown Prosecution Service. Grand juries tended to consist of 'gentlemen of high standing' who, in the case of Bury St Edmunds, would literally be the landed gentry. The electoral reform discussions of 1917 prompted the desire for the abolition of grand juries and their replacement by 'petty (from the French petit) juries consisting of twelve good men (and women after enfranchisement) and true' chosen from those entitled to vote. Jurors are still selected at random from the electoral register in the twenty-first century and a 'J' is placed beside their names if they are to be considered eligible for jury service.

In late January, the *Bury Free Press* reported that forty people had been killed in an ammunitions explosion, but then imposed a total news black-out and declined to say where this had occurred or to give any details. There were two small ammunitions workshops in Bury St Edmunds and a large ammunitions factory in Stowmarket some 15 miles away. The reasons for this secrecy are not clear, except to possibly prevent information from reaching the enemy. However, when 5 tons of TNT exploded at a munitions factory in Ashton-under-Lyne later that year, killing a similar number, injuring hundreds, and doing immense damage to the town, it was widely reported with messages of sympathy from the king and queen and mass funerals for the victims. The reason may simply have been that Bury St Edmunds was much nearer to the East Coast and more vulnerable to attack by Zeppelins than Ashton-under-Lyne, which lies on the western edge of the Pennines.

Winter this year was bitterly cold with snow and many degrees of frost. Bury St Edmunds and West Suffolk, being part of East Anglia, which is one of the coldest and driest parts of England, registered up to 36 degrees of frost in mid-February, only surpassed by Market Harborough in Leicestershire, which registered 39 degrees of frost on 4 February. Folk shivered with coal shortages and trying to conserve usage of gas and electricity due to rising prices. Bury Gas Company, however, had enjoyed a good year and had invested well in war loan stock. Train services were also curtailed to economise on coal. To partly recompense soldiers and sailors travelling on railways bedevilled by altered timetables and reduced train services, Great Eastern Railway offered free buffets and tearooms to those in military uniform. Meanwhile, the Suffolk Sheep Society was thriving and contributing to the war loans scheme. The Ministry of Munitions gave permission for the Suffolk Agricultural Show to go ahead in the summer of 1917, providing that only livestock was shown. Cattle, sheep and a dwindling number of horses would be eligible. The ladies' representative on the West Suffolk War Agriculture Committee proposed a scheme for a greater production of jam by small fruit farmers. The problem, however, was not so much the fruit production as the growing scarcity of sugar, and there was talk of a committee for overseeing sugar distribution. There seemed to be a committee for everything: war savings; war produce; war agriculture; war bonus allowances; war pensions; war tribunals; war economy; war food and fuel, etc, in addition to all the traditional municipal, civic and voluntary committees already established, and some were getting very tired of committees. It was a cry that echoed around the country.

War casualties were now practically a daily event and weekly lists were published in the *Free Press*. Individuals were making incredible patriotic contributions, one local family having nine sons in the forces, another had five sons serving, and one Bury St Edmunds lady reported that of her four sons in the war, two were dead, one was an injured prisoner-of-war, and one was still serving. All over the country the war machine was swallowing the menfolk in their tens of thousands, so the War Office was also recruiting women for the army, as clerks and typists, cooks and motor transport drivers, storehouse keepers and checkers, telephone and postal workers, etc. In addition there were 100,000 female land workers nationally. The intention was to free-up men to fight at the Front by replacing them with women in auxiliary jobs. Employers had to furnish labour returns to be sent to the military authorities under the terms of DORA. Drivers, motor fitters, turners, smiths, store-keepers and students were urgently needed by the Army Recruiting Office at the barracks in Bury. The war was costing the country an unprecedented and enormous amount of money every day, and there was great pressure to economise in every way and maximise savings. Due to the paper shortage, large posters, circulars and catalogues were banned. The Red Cross and the Boy Scouts organised collections of waste paper for recycling. Public transport services were curtailed, especially at holiday times. New restrictions were placed on bread and the selling of bread. Bread was not to be sold until it was at least twelve hours old. There were no routine slicing machines. Loaves were sold uncut and very fresh bread was difficult to cut into thin slices with a carving or bread knife.

New bread was not to be exchanged for older bread. Currant, sultana or milk bread was prohibited. No sugar was to be used in baking bread. Loaves were to be either one piece oven bottom loaves, tin loaves, or rolls. Bread had to be sold by weight either 1lb (500g) or even numbers of pound weights, and rolls had to weigh 2oz (about 63g). The only exceptions to these rules was to be bread sold in cafés or restaurants. Lord Devonport issued a serious warning that food prices must not rise more or the food controller would issue strict regulations. Pensioners in particular were not faring well. They received no pension until they were 70 years of age. It was stated that any Friendly Society benefits they received should not be counted as income, but a war bonus of only 2s.6d (£6.25) per pensioner was granted.

Although Bury St Edmunds had not suffered food shortages quite as badly as some places, due to the town being at the heart of a rural farming community, David Lloyd George had issued a national statement that food stocks were now seriously depleted and sailors were dying in increasing numbers in an attempt to provide food as merchant shipping was constantly being attacked by the German Navy. Therefore, a scheme was devised whereby all men who had been born and bred in the countryside, although they might now be living or working in towns and cities, and who were not eligible for military service, would spearhead a self-help campaign. Therefore, any who had offered the following services could also offer to help grow the necessary foodstuffs:

- amateur/professional gardeners
- flower growers
- brickyard hands
- livery stablemen
- road menders
- water pipe layers
- golf club employees
- outdoor servants
- gamekeepers
- hedgers and ditchers
- ex ploughmen
- any who had worked on the land

This would not be a problem for a town like Bury but, in addition, up to 500,000 men nationally were wanted immediately for National

Service in agriculture, woodlands, shipbuilding, building construction and engineering, and all men aged 18–61 were to be encouraged, not to say exhorted, to enrol for National Service. 'A man who will not help his country is helping the enemy.' The Archdeacon of Lincoln, speaking at Llangollen in Wales, tried to provide an upbeat note about all the suffering and casualties, the endless regulations and privations being endured:

> We needed the Great War to save us from the utmost damnation, for there was a greater peril in the direction we were going ... as a people, luxury, materialism and social inequity were consuming us when God, in His mercy, smote us! If the war had ended in the first six months ... we should have become the rottenest nation the world had ever known ... three years ago we worshipped riches ... the nation was now finding itself in what Ruskin called the rough school of war.

The *Bury Free Press* dutifully reported his speech without much enthusiasm. Many of its readers were grieving family losses. There was a great deal of rural poverty and social inequity still. Profiteering was affecting and intensely annoying everyone. The rough school of war was doing little to help anyone, despite everyone's efforts. The punishment seemed to have outweighed the crime. However, if revenge is a dish best eaten cold, the *Free Press* must have felt a twinge of satisfaction as it reported the death of Count Zeppelin at Charlottenburg near Berlin. He, whose flying machines had introduced the terror of death from the skies, and had so frightened Bury St Edmunds folk, was no more. However, the Zeppelin raids were greatly decreasing and the town now had a 'brazen-throated buzzer' of an air-raid siren.

In early March, the Russian Revolution began. Tsar Nicolas II had been held personally responsible by Russian folk for the huge losses sustained by the Russian army in the Great War. The 'White Russians', who were loyal to the tsar, were finally defeated by the Bolsheviks or the 'Red Russians'. The tsar was then deposed and imprisoned with his family at Ykaterinburg. King George V and Tsar Nicolas were cousins who bore an uncanny physical resemblance to each other. Privately, the two men had always been friendly and Nicolas was confident that George would grant him and his family the political asylum he requested. Unfortunately that was not to be the case. On a personal level, the king had little hesitation about complying with his cousin's request, but he was uneasy about the view the Establishment would take of his gesture and, more than that, he was very worried that if he granted the tsar asylum, it might encourage Englishmen, fed up with austerity plus all the pomp and circumstance of royalty, to rebel in the same way that the Russian working classes had done. Reluctantly, therefore, he turned down the tsar's request. The following summer the tsar and his family would be executed by the Bolsheviks. The Russian Revolution was ultimately responsible for Russia withdrawing from the Great War in October 1917. It proved a blow to the Allies, made worse by the fact that much Russian weaponry was sold to the Germans.

King George was now forced to consider other family problems. He was facing the embarrassing prospect of continuing to fight another of his cousins, Kaiser Wilhelm, with whom he had got on rather well before the war. After the tragedy of the Somme, anti-German feeling was running extremely high in Britain and he felt that it was just too much to ask the British people to follow and fight for a king of German descent and bearing the very German name of Saxe-Coburg-Gotha. George V couldn't help his lineage, but he could make a very public gesture of renouncing his German connections. On 17 July 1917, he issued a royal proclamation:

> Now, therefore, We, out of Our Royal Will and Authority, do hereby declare and announce that as from the date of this Our Royal Proclamation, Our House and Family shall be styled and known as the House and Family of Windsor, and that all the descendants in the male line of Our said Grandmother, Queen Victoria, who are subjects of this realm ... shall bear the said Name of Windsor.

Food and its production had become the most important matter, especially for rural areas and farming towns like Bury St Edmunds that served them. The authorities commandeered farms that they said were being 'cultivated improperly' because billeting or accommodation for soldiers and other folk working the land was urgently needed. There were complaints about ploughing standards and many seed potatoes were lost to the harsh frosts of 1917's winter. David Lloyd George insisted on a minimum weekly wage of 25/- (£62.50) for agricultural labourers, the same pay as those working under the National Service scheme. A smallholdings scheme for discharged soldiers began to take shape and allotments were proving popular. By Easter there were thirty-eight allotments in Grove Road, twenty-eight in Hospital Road and fourteen in Hollow Road. Sixty allotments and 10 rods were to be let on land to the south of Boby's Klondyke Works. A rod (perch or pole as it is also known) is a unit of length equal to 5.5yds or 16.5ft (5.03m). One Bury St Edmunds landlord gave each of his tenants a portion of meadow near their homes, rent free, for growing vegetables. Pheasants were doing a lot of damage to farms and crops and it was advocated that they should be shot with the bonus of providing a tasty addition to the pot. Local rats were also having a field-day taking advantage of the growing food to such an extent that the authorities were willing to pay reasonable rates to those able to hunt them down and kill them. Local churchmen argued about the merits of working the allotments on Sundays, but the Bishop of Lincoln silenced their protests, justifying Sunday working as the Christian spirit helping men in times of war. The need for food was paramount and the allotments were 'a work of charity and necessity'.

The *Bury Free Press* began publishing recipes as part of a cookery economy drive. Some, like nut rissoles, vegetable hotpot or lentil and rice cutlets, will be familiar to modern vegetarians. Nettles were used for soup or as a vegetable. Barley, maize and even turnips were advocated as alternatives for making bread. Turnip bread was said to taste similar to bread made from wheat. Around Bury St Edmunds and the local West Suffolk villages there would usually be a rabbit or bird to add to the pot as well. One or two other official suggestions, like fried porridge scones, were generally shunned, and one alternative for a second vegetable was just plain inedible. Cooks were advised to boil stale bread, potato peelings and old vegetable leaves together and then mash them through a sieve to give an unappetising brown puree.

Despite the food shortages, numbers of hounds for hunting continued to be kept and fed, causing widespread protest. There was, however, an eggs and poultry industry development in East Anglia, spearheaded by the Great Eastern Railway poultry train, which toured the eastern counties encouraging support for the fledgling business. Framlingham and Eastern Counties Eggs & Poultry Co-operative Society had undertaken the collection and marketing of eggs and poultry for Suffolk, Norfolk, Essex and Cambridgeshire. In a single year they handled 15,500,000 eggs. Shares in the company were 5/- (£12.50) each and 5 per cent interest was paid. Elmswell Bacon Factory, a few miles from Bury St Edmunds, won great praise for the quality and output of its bacon. However, there were now general meat shortages and Bury St Edmund's market day on Wednesdays was designated a meatless day, causing great local outrage. Fish was allowed, though, so hotels and restaurants could put together menus featuring soup, a main fish entree and a pudding. The Suffolk Hotel in Bury served a four course meal of soup, then Scotch salmon with potatoes, cucumber and sauce followed by preserved plums and blancmange, finishing with cheese and celery.

Thingoe petty sessions, just before Easter, raised smiles when a witness in a case stated that Suffolk folk had low intelligence, hence the nickname of 'silly Suffolk'. Someone had to explain to him gently that 'silly' actually meant 'holy' and that Suffolk folk were very religious. As Easter approached, services were held in the local churches and there was a special service in the cathedral to dedicate war shrines in honour of the fallen, although some folk objected to the shrines as a 'frivolous imitation of Rome'. There was also a special service for nursing staff. A number of entertainments were provided over the Easter period and some 'pretty military weddings' took place. Easter Monday was for sports and football matches. The matron of West Suffolk General Hospital received the Royal Red Cross awarded by the king for military nursing services to wounded soldiers in Bury. However, the question uppermost in everyone's mind now was the production of food. In May the king issued a proclamation that was read out by the mayor and asked people:

> ... to reduce the consumption of bread in their respective families by at least one fourth of the quantity consumed in ordinary times ... and to abstain from the use of flour in pastry ...

It was also advised that folk should limit themselves to one large slice of bread per day and to reduce the cakes, biscuits and tarts that they either bought or baked at home. The king was adamant that his own family should also follow the restrictions and royal cooks were instructed to be extremely parsimonious in accordance with his wishes.

It was suggested that the water meadows of the pretty River Lark, which flows through Bury St Edmunds, should be used for growing rye, but the agricultural committee were faced with the problem of the 'Lark torrent', which meant that the water meadows were prone to flooding. All rivers have water meadows to take excess water when the river is high through heavy rains, but many are either cultivated

West Suffolk Hospital, Bury St Edmunds, *c.*1915.

or built-up, and this causes any excess water to flood a wider area. The River Lark was in bad condition, having silted up due to poor maintenance as a result of war economy measures. Bury St Edmunds had quite a lot of low lying land, many timbered medieval buildings, and a population that did not want to see their town under water. Local farmers complained that the military had commandeered their stocks of hay at £5.2s.6d (£256.25) per ton, but that purchases of alternative feeding stuffs for animals was more expensive. Cotton-cake was £16 (£800) per ton and linseed cake was £20 (£1,000) per ton. The farmers saw this discrepancy as a war tax upon themselves. Not as many root crops were grown due to labour shortages. This was unfortunate since the roots of mangolds, or mangel-wurzels as they are better known, are a cheap nutritious alternative for feeding cattle and pigs, while the leaves can be lightly cooked and used as a vegetable or in salads. Mangolds need to be grown in well-dug, well-composted soil and watered regularly, a task female land workers could have undertaken had they been allowed to do so. There was also concern about sufficient feed and grazing being available for working horses, but they were becoming much fewer in number as the military authorities commandeered them for the fighting. The best option available for farmers was to club together to purchase farm machinery that could be shared and would do the work of both horses and labourers, but there was a reluctance on the part of many to take this step. West Suffolk pasture and grasslands were ordered to be ploughed up to grow food. There had been 11,000,000 acres of arable land in 1915 and this needed to be increased to 15,000,000 acres by 1918. Farmers quarrelled over the worth of arable land and pasture, and claiming compensation. Landowners and landlords felt they were also entitled to consideration if use of their land was to be changed. Maintenance costs would increase, but they were not allowed to raise rents. The government pointed out that no animal feedstuffs would be imported in 1918, so all farmers would need to grow their own, that the country was at war and in a very serious situation regarding feeding people and animals alike, and that things could either be done voluntarily or under DORA regulations. No one mentioned that if farmers had previously been flexible enough to take female labour, prisoner-of-war labour, Irish farm labour, or boy scout labour when it was offered, the situation might not have been quite so serious, but the undertones were there, reflected in the government's firm non-negotiable stance. The farmers took a simpler view. It was not their war so why should they have to pay for it? It was a difficult situation for everyone, but the paramount need was to become self-sufficient so that the German plan of starving Britain into submission would fail.

War casualties continued to rise and the controversy over war shrines raged on. Bury St Edmunds determined to celebrate Empire Day again, war or no war, with processions and events on Angel Hill. There was, after all, little enough to celebrate generally, and there was a subdued crowd in the Abbey Gardens on Whit Monday. School treats were deemed inadvisable this year. Racing was banned, which badly affected nearby Newmarket, and the Derby was cancelled. German princes were now to be banned from the House of Lords, depriving them of their legal right to sit there and rescinding their pensions. However, the move was proving both awkward and difficult and there was the uncomfortable fact that both the king and queen came from this same class.

For 200 years, since George I had ascended the throne in 1714, there had been only German royal blood in the main line of the English royal family with the sole exception of Queen Alexandra, the wife of Edward VII. She was Danish but closely allied to the German aristocracy. The US had now entered the war after the Germans decided to attack all ships bound for Britain, which would inevitably include US ships, and the Germans had also offered an alliance to Mexico. Having America on board was an important morale booster for the Allies and raised hopes that perhaps the end really was in sight.

There were now 1,000 Suffolk prisoners-of-war held in Germany. Bury St Edmunds workers helped in the task of sending them three food parcels per fortnight, each parcel weighing 10lb (about 5kg), and 6lb (just under 3kg) of bread per week. A parcel of tobacco and cigarettes was sent once a fortnight and supplies of clothing every six months. Appeals were made for books, papers and magazines that had been requested both by troops fighting abroad and by the YMCA for their soldiers' and sailors' recreation huts. Fêtes and flag days and sales were held by the Red Cross or local organisations in Bury to raise funds for these supplies. Bury special constables, who had a generally hard time of it, not being much respected by the public and given all the 'dirty jobs' to do, were delighted to win a tug of war with VTC and VAD teams after jousting with them during a Red Cross fête day sports session. However, there was always someone to find fault and complaints were made that flag-day sales girls taking money from men would 'lead to evil ways'. This was ignored by the Red Cross and most sensible folk. Suffolk Red Cross was helping on all fronts and raised a total of £53,000 (£2,653,000).

The National Association of discharged Soldiers and Sailors held meetings in Bury aimed at finding suitable employment for ex-servicemen and securing more adequate pension allowances. However, food and food economy had become the main issues affecting Bury St Edmunds and its surrounding villages. The hoarding of food and profiteering all over the country was leading towards food control and rationing in order to ensure fair shares for everyone and to put an end to the avaricious greed of a comparative few. A national food economy campaign was initiated and a food control officer appointed for Bury under DORA regulations.

The *Bury Free Press* was printing food economy recipes each week. Treats included liver and lentil savoury, barley pudding and maize scones. Those growing food faced several problems. Pheasants were becoming a serious nuisance, rabbits were destroying crops and trees, cabbage moths and caterpillars were attacking young plants, and there were the ever present rats always ready to take advantage of anything they could lay their paws on and eat. The Destruction of Pheasants Order was revived and it was legal once again to shoot them. Pheasants were a good source of meat and doubtless the order was very welcome, if not to the pheasants. Named persons could also apply for orders to 'kill and take rabbits', and anyone was allowed to kill rats. Payment of 2d or 3d (40p or 60p) might be offered per dozen tails (proof of the rats' demise). The new food controller appealed to folk to eat less, especially bread and sugar. There was a theft of asparagus, lettuce and spring cabbage from the Spring Lane allotments, which was condemned as beyond despicable. Despite controversy over whether potatoes should be sprayed or not, Bury St Edmunds Council bought two spraying machines. Although the situation had not yet reached the point where every potato counted it was close, and a bad potato harvest could not be afforded. To assist the food economy drive, Olivers' grocers on Abbeygate Street announced that their store would close at 2.00pm on Mondays, Tuesdays and Fridays as well as a half-day on Thursdays. Wednesdays and Saturdays, both market days, would be the only days when the store would remain open all day. The food controller was also responsible for fuel and there was talk of purchasing large quantities of coal so that there would be a stock from which the poor could buy coal in winter. It was a good idea, but impractical and virtually impossible as supplies of coal had dwindled nationally owing to insufficient numbers of miners and much of the available coal supplies being shipped to the Front for Allied needs, as well as being used for shipping and munitions works.

The women of the town tried to take their minds off all the problems by holding a Baby Week at the end of July. The new generation was being hailed as of utmost importance for replacing the hundreds of thousands who had died in the carnage of trench warfare and Gallipoli. There were public meetings, film shows, a garden party, pram parade and a baby show. The whole venture was a big success, but then it was back to queueing at the shops for dwindling supplies, or making lentil curries, pease pudding and apricot jam without sugar. The men were consumed by the inequities of compulsory conscription, the ruination of small businesses and sole proprietorships when key personnel were called-up, and the military tribunals dealing with appeals. The need for more and more cannon fodder was so great that comparatively few appeals were allowed. One-man businesses were suffering badly and so was agriculture. Some men, young or older, married or single, had more responsibilities and commitments than others. Homes were broken up as wage earners had to join the forces. Bury St Edmunds military tribunals were reasonably sympathetic, but they were under pressure to supply manpower to the Front. Suffolk County appeal tribunals said that certain local needs were necessary in rural areas, such as carriers of goods, but the general government line was that everyone had to make sacrifices. 'We're all in this together' became a favourite catchphrase, although in this case even government members joined in and many MPs, notably the prime minister and the chancellor of the exchequer, gave up their parliamentary salaries for the duration of the war. The one category of appealers who drew little sympathy was that of conscientious objectors. A number agreed to take non-combative jobs in the medical and auxiliary services, or in the munitions factories, but some clung defiantly to their principles and refused to do anything connected in any way with the war. They were sent to prison for a time and then often given work on council/community projects since no one else would employ them.

There were just two divisions in West Suffolk under the new electoral reform and representation of the people bill passed in 1917, and Bury town lost its MP. The Bury St Edmunds division included the municipal borough of Bury and the urban district of Newmarket as well as areas north and west in the county including Brandon, Mildenhall, Moulton, Thedwastre RDC and some of Thingoe RDC. The Sudbury division included places to the south and east in the county, including the municipal borough of Sudbury, the urban districts of Glemsford, Hadleigh and Haverhill, numerous villages and that part of Thingoe RDC not included within the Bury division. However, the major reform was that the vote was now to be given to women over the age of 30. It was the suffragette dream come true and due to the simple fact that on the declaration of war they had laid aside their campaign for women to have the vote and thrown themselves wholeheartedly into the war effort. They did the jobs men did before going off to fight with equal aptitude, they provided back-up support to the forces, they cared for refugees, nursed the sick, raised funds for the troops and prisoners-of-war, brought up their children and kept the home fires burning. The Conservative home secretary, George Cave, introducing the new Representation of the People Act, said:

War by all classes of our countrymen has brought us nearer together, has opened men's eyes, and removed misunderstandings on all sides. It has made it, I think, impossible that ever again, at all events in the lifetime of the present generation, there should be a revival of the old class feeling which was responsible for so much, and, among other things, the exclusion for a period, of so many of our population from the class of electors.

One wit in the local Bury paper said there were three classes of society: aristocracy, snobocracy and democracy, and that finally democracy seemed to have triumphed.

The muted sounds of the guns in Flanders could be heard in Bury and on the third anniversary of the war, intercession services were held in local churches, but the major emphasis in people's minds now was the production of food, at reasonable prices with equal shares for everyone, so that the country would not starve and the German plan would be foiled. Recipes in the *Free Press* had begun relying heavily on barley, vermicelli rissoles and bean stew were advocated, boiled rice and raisins were a treat. There was a new bread order. Bacon pigs were fetching record prices. Then, at the height of the summer, there was an outbreak of anthrax at Honington, a village about 9.5 miles (16km) from Bury St Edmunds. Wood pigeons were making a nuisance of themselves eating grain and were shot like the pheasants and rabbits that were attacking fledgling crops. There were further war bonuses for the police, and pensioners were to receive additional small grants of between 2s 6d (£6.25) and 5/- (£12.50), but teachers' salaries were so low they could barely afford to eat bread and cheese in many cases. Even a head teacher could only earn £80–£100 (£4,000–£5,000) per annum. Some teachers earned as little as £50 (£2,500) a year. Agricultural wages were also very low, less than 25/- (£62.50) per week in many cases, and there were protests that resulted in members of the Farmers' Union locking out agricultural workers in the nearby villages of Fakenham, Honington and Euston. The county war pensions office was not making matters any easier. 'Efficiency, economy and satisfactory results were needed', which required 'time, attention and labour', and a good secretary was required even if it meant paying higher wages. Olivers' grocers were reporting tea shortages, although coffee was still in good supply but expensive, and everywhere was reporting a scarcity of sugar. There were also individuals stealing from allotments and gaining from other peoples' hard work, which prompted so much anger and resentment that a fine of £100 (£5,000) was levied on anyone who was caught.

The major event in the spring of 1917 had been the formation and recruitment drive for the Women's Land Army, which was part of the National Service scheme for war work. Women could apply and sign forms at their local post office. They would then be summoned to appear before a joint committee of employment exchange and district selection/allocation for interview. If accepted the woman underwent a medical examination and was then registered and placed under the care of the district village registrar for the village where she would work. Women entered at three levels:

- if sufficiently skilled, she would go straight to a farm as a paid worker
- if suitable, she received a 16/- (£40) per week bursary and was placed on a farm for training
- if she required four weeks basic training, she would go to a centre with expenses paid

There was also an appeal for males aged 18–61 to show patriotism and volunteer to form a male register of village workers who could be asked to undertake work of national importance anywhere in Britain. There would be a minimum wage of 25/- (just over £62) per week with a possible subsistence allowance.

Lord Rhondda, who was responsible at national level for food supplies and prices, was experiencing severe problems sourcing and maintaining all food supplies and their methods of distribution. Farmers were suffering as well from shortages of fertilisers, seeds and feeding stuffs, and they needed to secure their supplies of fertilisers, root seeds, seed potatoes, binder twine and land drain pipes for 1918 a year in advance.

Profiteering was causing massive problems. Supplies of various goods were withheld to force prices up and now that there was re-frigeration this could be applied to meat and other perishable food-stuffs. This wasn't just a local problem, it was a national problem. But a few got very rich at the expense of many and it was making people extremely angry. So too was the hoarding of food by those who could afford to buy more than they needed, which left less for everyone else. Pleas for voluntary regulation fell on deaf ears and, in the end, the government was left with no option but to enforce regulation by law under the terms of DORA. At the beginning of September it was announced that sugar rationing would begin at the end of December. Sugar cards would be needed to obtain any supplies of sugar and registration was to begin immediately. This was followed by a Cheap Meat Order, which fixed meat prices at 1s.1d (around £2.70) per pound weight (250g) for butchers, and consumers were to benefit from a 2d (approximately 40p) reduction per pound weight (250g). The problem from the butchers' point of view was that they had to pay for whole carcasses, including bones, but as customers didn't want to pay for bones, it meant a considerable decrease in their profits. By mid-September a standard loaf of bread was on sale at a regulated price of 9d (£1.80). Milk deliveries were reduced and milk prices were fixed, both of which created a great deal of controversy. The food controller had a difficult brief deciding the prices and methods of distribution while maintaining national economy in their consumption, and took as a base-line the cost of production plus a fair profit. Farmers felt, with some justification, that in view of the rising costs of animal feedstuffs, they were losing out on meat and milk products. In addition, there was to be a controlled coal distribution for the coming winter, so that rapidly dwindling stocks would be shared out evenly, and this would also be overseen by the food controller. The wool department at the War Office agreed to fix clothing prices so that poorer folk could afford to buy clothes. The main problem here was that shortages of new wool were caused by military requirements, and this resulted in excessive price rises. Certain maximum costs were laid down for tailoring as well. This didn't stop John Field of Bury St Edmunds attempting to sell: 'fur wear of quality, slumber-wear of cosiness [winceyette]; blouse wear for beauty and neck wear of the moment.' Bury St Edmunds was, however, and still is, both a 'County town' and a 'county town.' In other words it was the 'capital' of West Suffolk and it also catered for county landowners and the local aristocracy as well as for working class folk. A whist drive was held in the town just before Christmas in aid of the Suffolk wool fund and raised nearly £50 (£2,500).

Casualties and the numbers of prisoners-of-war continued to rise rapidly. Suffolk Prisoner-of-War Fund held street collections, stalls, a fête and a football match between two teams of female munitions workers, raising over £1,230 (£61,650). A white elephant rummage sale at the Corn Exchange in Bury raised £171 (£8,558). Female football matches raised great interest. The mayor kicked-off two matches between teams of female munitions workers and teams of male players who had their right hands tied behind their backs. The first team, led by Rose Manning, won 3–0, and the second team, led by Rose Shorter, won 7–4. Wounded troops were not forgotten either. Public baths for soldiers were built in the cattle market and the month of October was set aside for special help for sailors. 'Pansy days' were held in Bury for the benefit of sailors. The name means 'thought' and the flower was seen as a colourful symbol of free thought. However, the council decided to charge the War Office £28 (about £1,400) per annum for use of the cricket field after £90 worth (just over £4,500) of damage was caused by troops using it as a drill ground. The Isolation Hospital was having a difficult time but was coping well with several notifiable infectious diseases, which included enteric fever (typhoid), scarlet fever, diphtheria, polio, erysipelas (also known as holy fire, it is an acute skin infection), measles and German measles. Unlike many other parts of the country, TB cases were low. The infant mortality rate was 96 per 1,000 – low by the standards of the time. The importance of hygiene and public health was beginning to be recognised. Young mothers were educated in how best to care for their babies. Sanitation for dairies, to prevent contamination of milk by flies and dust, and the cleanliness of conditions for milk, butter and cream, were assessed. The ventilation, drainage, water supply, lighting and cleanliness of slaughterhouses and the deposits of dirt on floors and storage of fuel, with its attendant coal dust, in bakeries were also being studied with a view to improvement. However, one of the biggest problems was the cramped, sometimes squalid, conditions of workers' houses in the town and farm labourers' cottages in the country, but this was not currently being addressed and no closing orders of housing unfit for human habitation were made.

Lighting issues were still giving Bury grief. The DORA restrictions remained in force and there were numerous accidents. A number of folk wanted prams to carry red warning lights like bicycles, and a few even suggested they should have a horn or a bell as well. There were also several assaults and 'molestations' in the dark, especially upon women. Finally it was decided that all lamps in Bury should be blue, like the air-raid warning lamps. They would give a little light but would not be easily visible from above. In any case, Zeppelin raids had virtually ceased, mainly due to the fact that planes and anti-aircraft guns had learned how to successfully shoot them down. But

Bury was still suffering from post-traumatic stress after the raids earlier in the war and townsfolk were reluctant to believe that they were more or less safe from aerial bombing.

There was now the question of 750,000 returning soldiers who were anxious for re-settlement on the land. Suffolk had plenty of available agricultural land. However, British farming and food production methods were behind those of Britain's continental neighbours. The land was just as good, if not better in many cases, but whereas German farmers could feed seventy to seventy-five persons per acre, British farmers could only feed forty-five to fifty per acre. Their gross receipts per unit of cultivated land was only one-fifth those of Belgium and two-thirds those of Denmark. Another problem was that an extra 200,000 new houses would be needed in the aftermath of the war to accommodate those returning to 'a land fit for heroes'. Meanwhile, the development of the eggs and poultry industry in East Anglia as a whole was going well and a 'fattening farm' for poultry destined for the table was established. Manchester and Sheffield asked for egg supplies, but unfortunately the carriage proved too expensive. The Food Production Department had made available 2,000 tractors for all English and Welsh farmers, but many farmers were not mechanically minded and still preferred the old fashioned methods. A further restriction order was published for wheat and rye, prohibiting their use as animal foodstuffs for, despite the shortages, animals and poultry were still being fed on grain. Under DORA, a further restriction was added. No seed mustard was to be grown in West Suffolk in 1918 without a certificate from West Suffolk County War Agricultural Committee. There were more meat and bread shortages and some difficulties in fixing coal prices were experienced. Gas and electricity prices continued to rise steadily.

As Christmas approached, the Department of Food Economy at the Ministry of Food issued a statement to the press that the use of dried fruit in Christmas cooking should be severely restricted and sugar was to be replaced by treacle. Barley kernels were advocated as a good substitute for rice. Christmas meat prices, especially those of beef and mutton, were fixed. Butchers put on seasonal displays and so did other traders. There were lots of Christmas advertisements and another new series of Raphael Tuck Christmas cards and novelties, but it was a subdued Christmas celebrated quietly. There were the usual church services and carol concerts and the Theatre Royal

staged a performance of *Betty*. Snow fell and it was a 'white Christmas' but cold. Christmas dinners were provided but on a rather more
modest scale than in previous years, although pheasants, rabbits and
plenty of home-grown vegetables helped to make it more festive than
in many northern towns. There were snowball fights and a football
'carnival' on Boxing Day, but at the back of everyone's mind was
great weariness and a single thought. When will this war ever end?

CHAPTER 5

1918

The New Year opened with intercession services held on the first Sunday and the settlement of a strike at Cornish & Lloyds, an iron foundry on Risbygate Street. The strike had been handled by the Workers' Union and concerned demands for an extra £1 (approx £45) on pre-war wages plus 12.5 per cent for a fifty-hour week. Such strikes caused tension and, in some cases, bad feeling. There was a war on, said some, surely it was unpatriotic to strike. On the other hand the cost of living had risen so much and so rapidly that many workers were struggling to feed their families and pay rent to keep a roof over their heads. Others received war bonuses to help them manage, but not everyone was so fortunate. The people most irked by the strike were Bury soldiers serving at the Front. They read the *Bury Free Press* sent from home as a way of keeping in touch and, like their counterparts elsewhere in the country, were generally appalled by strikes. Some wrote to the newspaper. Soldiers and sailors could not go on strike. They would be shot for dereliction of duty. Soldiers' pay was lower than most other occupations and they had to operate under the most dreadful and deadly conditions, while those at home could work without fear and go home each night to the comfort of their homes. Ironically, soldiers and sailors did not receive war bonuses. In a further irony the Theatre Royal chose this time to stage a comedy revue entitled *Blighty*, which is a corruption of the Hindu word for home.

The winter promised to be long, cold and severe. The countryside shivered under snow and frost. It was perhaps not the best of times to give speeches advocating birth control, but it had to be admitted that birth control reduced poverty, squalor, over-crowding and 'the misery of over-maternity'. The families of doctors, teachers and clergymen had the lowest birth rates, an indication that maybe education was a contributory factor. There was talk of educational reform after the war and of further education schemes after 'day schooling' had ended, for the war had shown 'that young men and women must no longer be regarded simply as units in an industrial machine'. As if to give an alternative way of keeping warm other than cuddling up, Sir Ernest Clarke published a 300-year-old recipe for turtle soup held at Cupola House in the Traverse. The main problem with Sir Ernest's publication was the lack of turtles available in Bury St Edmunds. Back in the real world it was announced that potato flour was to be used in bread-making and that there were national shortages of beef and pork, but not in Bury St Edmunds. It was, after all, a country town. Amazingly, imported meat was still cheaper than home-killed meat by up to 3d (approximately 57p) per pound (500g) weight. There were protests over shortages of feedstuffs for the production of meat and milk, and at the Ministry of Food, fixing maximum retail prices at less than first-hand wholesale prices and excluding foreign imports from fixed-pricing policies. Suffolk sheep were still extremely popular, however, and there was a scheme afoot for West Suffolk farmers to grow flax. Flax was required for aeroplane construction and 3,000 acres of it were necessary. This scheme was complemented by a request in early March for Bury Businessmen's Week to raise sufficient funds to pay for seventeen planes. Sugar was now rationed and those without sugar ration cards were not allowed any supplies. It was also obvious that there was going to be further rationing, particularly of tea, butter, margarine and bacon. Pawseys Stores on St Johns Street were selling nine varieties of 'soup squares' at 2d (38p) a time which was probably one of the cheapest food options available. A seed merchant who had a stall on the Bury Wednesday market was doing a great trade with a wide selection of vegetable seeds. Seed potatoes, onions, parsnips and haricot beans were popular for allotments and the Klondyke allotments were doing particularly well.

The local special constables who had replaced the policemen enlisting in the forces were still a thorn in the side of the general public in the town and were being given a hard time by many who simply regarded them as imposters. They were regularly sworn at and verbally abused and sometimes hit by those for whom they were trying to keep law and order. One Bury St Edmunds householder insisted that even their cat was affected by the hatred and controversy, so much so that it 'ate the special constable's best canary!' The whole matter was not helped by the issue of further war bonuses to the constables. However the 'Specials' staged a concert at the

Theatre Royal to raise funds for the police orphanage and Bury St Edmunds Hospital. They raised £74 8.10d (approximately £3,240), which mollified some of these critics.

Winter seemed to have ended and early March saw a profusion of primroses, violets and daisies in bloom, lifting spirits a little and bringing renewed hope that this year would finally see the end of this dreadful war. Bury St Edmunds was praised for the quality of its 'good clear drinking water which has great organic purity and excellent quality'. The town also received the accolade of having invested £3,863 13s 8d (approximately £193,400) in the highest number of war savings certificates for the whole of Suffolk during the last quarter of 1917. The town council was criticised for refusing to have their minutes printed on both sides of paper, despite the paper shortage. The *Bury Free Press* opened a waste paper depot in the Shambles. School attendances increased and local teachers were debating whether to affiliate to Bury St Edmunds Labour Party. It was decided that illegitimate children should benefit under the Workmen's Compensation Act if they were dependent and would receive 7s.6d (£16.50) each. Illegitimacy was a huge stigma at this time, so the decision was very bold. The Theatre Royal surprised everyone by staging a controversial play, *Damaged Goods*, by the French dramatist Eugene Brieux, which tackled the subject of the 'hidden plague' of venereal diseases (VD – notably syphilis), now probably more colloquially known as sexually transmitted diseases (STDs). It was described as 'the play of the moment, a great play on social evil' and was for adults only. The war had highlighted the problems of VD (as such diseases were then known) and isolation hospitals dealt with numbers of soldiers who had returned from the Front having contracted syphilis. Cambridge had two hospitals dedicated to dealing with VD.

There were queues in the town for available supplies of tea and margarine and there were numerous complaints that the difficulty of long shopping queues was making children late for school. Agricultural workers were now to be paid on Fridays instead of Saturdays, so that their wives would have time to shop properly for the weekend. Onions, cabbages and leeks were grown on allotments, but the big patriotic call was for potatoes. Figures were published to show that in 1917 Suffolk had produced 24,500 tons of potatoes but had consumed 42,400 tons. That left a deficit of 17,900 tons and, heeding Lord Rhondda's appeals for self-sufficiency, the deficit had to be grown locally. Ideal crops to be grown in the 'shady borders' of allotments included artichokes, rhubarb, parsnips, cabbage, beetroot, kale, horse-radish, spinach and lettuce. Sugar-beet had been found to be a perfect food for pigs. Registration was taking place for rations of tea, butter and margarine, as well as meat, poultry, bacon and sausages. Fish remained unrationed but advance ordering was advised. Pawseys Grocers at 36 St Johns' Street took it upon themselves to publish an A–Z of unrationed foods, which they helpfully pasted up in their store to assist shoppers:

A   arrowroot, almonds
B   barley kernels, butter beans, bun flour, baking powder, baked beans (tinned)
C   cocoa, cornflour, custard powder, tinned fish
D   dates, damson jellies
E   eggs, but they cost 3½d (approximately 18.5p) each
F   flaked rice, flour (self raising)
G   ground rice, ground almonds, grapenuts, ground ginger, gelatine
H   haricot beans
I   isinglass (a substitute for gelatine)
J   jellies
K   kidney soup
L   lentils
M   maize flour
N   nutmegs
O   Oxo, onions, oysters
P   pea flour, peas, pearl barley
Q   Quaker oats
R   rice
S   soups, semolina, salmon, sardines, sage
T   tapioca, tuna fish
U   unsweetened milk
V   vegetables
W   walnuts, wheat semolina
Y   yellow split peas
Z   zest – to buy!

In April, the Great War budget was published. Flat rate income tax and super tax were both raised, and farmers were taxed under Schedule D for self-employed workers. Postage on cards and letters increased and so too did stamp duty on cheques. The prices of beer, spirits, tobacco and matches also increased, particularly spirits. The price of sugar increased by 1½d (approximately 29p) per pound weight (500g) and a tax was imposed on luxury establishments, luxury articles and jewellery. Even the cost of the *Bury Free Press* rose to 2d (about 38p). Still reeling from rising prices and rationing, folk were then informed that under DORA regulations they were not allowed to pick any gooseberries before 1 June. Punch drunk with rules and regulations, several townsfolk complained that the clock on St Marys' Church was slow and this was causing them to miss trains. The clock on Moyse's Hall, the medieval Jewish merchant's house in the centre of town, however, was very accurate. The matter of the two clocks caused a great deal of debate and several complaints, but it provided something on which to focus that didn't constantly remind people of the war.

The manpower situation was becoming critical. The Military Services Act of 1918 decreed that lists of all men of military age, no matter what their occupation, or whether it was graded, starred or unstarred, were to be submitted to the authorities. A special notice was sent to farmers that these lists were to include:

- farmers and market gardeners
- agricultural workers of all categories
- agricultural blacksmiths, farriers, wheelwrights
- experts/heads of department in wholesale food seed industry and forest tree nurseries
- managers, foremen, skilled workers in agricultural drainage
- retail harness makers and repairers
- land agents and administrators

Farmers would, however, have some say in who should be released and who should be retained, but the whole matter was to be settled by 3 June. Many farmers felt that this was a double whammy since they felt that food control and fixed prices were already adversely affecting them in many cases, and now key workers were to be taken as well. The tribunals were already back at work and there were numerous protests at the calling-up system with this fresh wave of conscription. Meanwhile, the sad lists of war casualties continued to grow, but there were bright spots with news of military awards for gallantry in the field, and the increase in war weddings continued. The *Bury Free Press* raised an extra smile with a report that the Turks considered

English prisoners-of-war rather odd for playing mouth organs and football by way of recreation.

Registration for sugar, butter and margarine rations had already taken place. Now it was the turn of tea. Meat coupons were issued separately. Bury and its surrounding villages were not as adversely affected by meat rationing as other places because the inhabitants had a legal right to shoot pheasants, rabbits and pigeons to protect crops. A hundred years on, pheasant is regarded as a luxury food, but rabbit and pigeon generally have too strong a taste for modern palates. In 1918, however, anything was a welcome addition to the family food supplies. Milk prices were fixed and the summer retail price was to be 2s 4d (approximately £10.70) per gallon (just under 9 litres). The Food Control Committee organised demonstrations of cheese-making for farmers (although many probably already knew how to do it, the Food Control Committee wanted to expand home-production) and setting up pig clubs to encourage both farmers and individuals to keep pigs. The idea of food kitchens was discussed, although many thought them unnecessary. This was partly to do with pride. They were seen as a form of charity, despite customers paying for their food. The idea was to buy and cook food in bulk, which would be more economical and use less fuel than individuals doing it in their own homes. The Bury area had quite a number of wealthy inhabitants who considered that they didn't need such things as food kitchens, even if all the servants had gone and the lady of the house was having to do the work herself. In addition, because much of the area was rural, there would be carriage and transport difficulties. Nevertheless, the local food control committee put forward reports that were accepted in principle. Thieving from allotments had become a growing and unpleasant problem despite a fine of £100 (£4,400) if they were caught.

It was now June and the *Free Press* was full of hints for allotment holders on growing vegetables, marrows, shallots, tomatoes and strawberries. The Food Control Committee was preparing to issue extra rations of sugar for jam-making from 1 July. There were problems with large numbers of ration book applications, especially for meat, which had no address on them, meaning that they could not be delivered. Part of the reason for this was that people were moving around and doubling up with other family members as wage-earners were called-up and their families could no longer afford to stay in their former homes. This contrasted sharply with a full-page advertisement in the local paper at the end of May for Lindsey Brothers' new showroom for fur coats, which was opening on the corner of the Buttermarket and Higher Baxter Street. A real life 'tale of two cities'.

In late June, the *Free Press* carried a note of the death of Prince Victor Duleep Singh, the head of the royal house of the Punjab and the elder brother of Prince Freddie Duleep Singh. Prince Freddie, a member of the Royal Victorian Order, became Crown Prince of the Punjab on his brother's death. He loved West Suffolk, spending most of his life there and building a temple hidden in woodlands where he could pray and remember his homeland. Prince Freddie served in France for two years during the Great War and then on the General Staff. He died in 1926 which marked the end of Bury St Edmunds' personal connection with the tragic romance of colonial India.

The town, however, had more pressing matters to hand, not the least of which was the production of food. It was time to sow runner beans, cabbages, kale, sprouts, peas, carrots, marrows and cauliflowers. The local paper gave instructions on making hoes, rakes and seed-drills at home from bits of wood and metal. At the same time archaeologists working in nearby Thetford discovered tools made out of fossil sponges, which had been used in the pre-historic flint mines at Grimes Graves. Bury folk, not having any fossil sponges to hand, had to make do with what they could find in their back yards. Suffolk Institute of Archaeology met regularly in the town. 'We are what our past has made us' was their favourite premise. Many must have wondered exactly what in the past had made such a dreadful war, much of it fought in suffocating muddy trenches, causing so much suffering.

A radical proposal was put forward nationally that the separation scheme allowance should be extended to all mothers of young children after the war. It should be a state endowment of motherhood and not payments administered by the Poor Law Guardians. Payments were to begin before birth and continue until the child started school. The weekly allowance would then stop for the mother but continue for the child until the child left school. There would be some restrictions for unmarried mothers and illegitimate children. This proposal acknowledged the recognition that a generation had been lost to the war and needed to be replaced, but it would also attract the new female vote that would be tested for the first time in elections due to be held in December that year.

Despite the farmers' protests, the minimum wage for agricultural workers had now risen to 30/- (£66) for a fifty-four-hour week in summer and a forty-eight-hour week in winter. There were rates of overtime pay that included all Sunday working. Meanwhile, a public meeting held in the Corn Exchange demanded the immediate internment of enemy aliens that would preclude prisoners-of-war working on the land at harvest-time. Farmers were already angry at being forced to pay fixed wages for harvesting and demanded action. Much of the action they got was from the Women's Land Army, which now numbered over 100,000 women from all walks of life. The women had received a good basic training and were willing to work hard and learn. The government refused to repatriate soldiers to help with the harvest. In any case, they no longer had the numbers of men to do so.

There was a massive thunderstorm in the evening of 17 July, said to be the worst for fifty years, which caused 'floods and rushing torrents'. Coincidentally, it was also the day that the Bolsheviks executed the Russian Imperial Family. An omen, perhaps, for a week later the first cases of influenza were reported in the town. An intercessionary service was held on the fourth anniversary of the war, but this year it was different. There was an air of cautious optimism. There had been a series of successful counter-attacks on German forces and the Allies had finally seized the initiative. On 8 August all German troops were forced back to the Hindenburg Line – 'a black day for the German Army', said General Erich von Ludendorff. This heralded the beginning of the Hundred Days Offensive that would finally end the Great War. There was, however, 'to be no hugger-mugger peace; it must be a real peace'. Bury St Edmunds, however, had more immediate things on its mind. There had been protests to Lord Lee, the director general of food production, about ploughing up land to grow food and there were several calls for its suspension. Ordinary folk were more concerned with the harvest, bottling fruit and vegetables, and the locally developing flax industry. There were a number of flax farms in the Bury area, and in early August, 420 people spent a whole week flax-pulling. At the end of the week the flax camp in Bury gave 'a cordial dinner party' and then announced that workers would be staying on another week to help nearby Stowmarket flax growers with their harvest. There had been discussions about a flax mill being situated in Bury, and Almoners

Barn Farm in Southgate Street was bought for the purpose, but there were complaints about possible floods and 'the pungent brewery type smell, like a tannery ... the odour coming from the drying process after treatments', and so the new flax factory opened in Glemsford just over 13 miles (about 23km) from Bury.

Suffolk sheep were still doing well and fetching record prices. At the Suffolk Sheep Society's annual sale a ram lamb would fetch 300 guineas (a guinea was worth £1.1s, and at modern values 300 guineas were worth £13,700). Many were exported to Canada.

The Ancient Order of Foresters held its AGM in Bury, as usual. There was a good deal of general masonic influence in the town, largely due to its history and the nature of its livelihoods. Farmers had been troubled about thatching but found, to their amazement, that females working in the Land Army had become proficient in the art and were quite capable of fulfilling thatching work. The Post Office, which had taken on numerous extra duties during the war, now facilitated Lord Rhondda's rationing scheme posters and cards, which involved a great deal of hard work in the national organisation and distribution of cards, as well as paying out all the various allowances. In 1917, 19,000,000 sugar rationing cards and coupons had been distributed. In 1918, 30,000,000 other ration cards and 5,000,000 League of National Safety enrolment cards had been distributed; and 100,000,000 allowances had been paid out. It was an impressive performance. Sales of National War Bonds topped 1,000 million. Teachers' salaries were to practically double, but this still gave a top wage of only £280 (approximately £12,200) per annum. Smiles were raised by a notice in a local munitions factory advising workers that they should not smoke or light matches.

Rather belatedly the army had decided to pay a weekly allowance of 5/- (£11) to the parents and grandparents who had been dependent upon the wages of young unmarried soldiers before they had enlisted or been called-up. It wasn't much, but it would help to pay for food. The question of food, in one way or another, was still uppermost. Butter and margarine allowances were to increase in September on a 2:1 ratio. The weekly allowance per person would now be 2oz (63g) butter and 4oz (125g) margarine per week. The shortage of grain had come down to a stark choice in the case of barley. Should it be bread or beer? However, there were increasing alcohol sales restrictions across East Anglia due to incoming US servicemen and the fact that there was total prohibition of alcohol in the US. The price of blackberry jam was to be fixed. A silly situation had arisen. There was a good crop of blackberries in the hedgerows, but permission for folk to pick them from hedgerows on farmland was withheld so that much of the crop remained unharvested due to shortage of farm labour. Eventually, blackberry prices were fixed at around 4d (about 72p) per pound (500g) weight. Apple prices were also to be fixed and jam, honey, syrup and marmalade were to be rationed, although children would be allowed larger rations of jam. It was a grim time and even sweets fell victim to the sugar shortages. In addition there were serious coal deficiencies for the coming winter, partly due to the US Army, and the argument for national kitchens was greatly strengthened. More land was to be put to the plough, despite protests, and marketing surplus from allotments would be dealt with officially. A co-operative marketing society was what was needed, according to the *Free Press*. The final basic average food ration list for one adult worked out as:

2oz (63g) tea (approximately sixteen tea bags)

8oz (250g) sugar

4 pints (approximately 2 litres) milk

1 loaf (large brown, 2lb (1kg) in weight, which is that of an average large uncut loaf)

4oz (125g) butter (later 6oz in total: 125g of margarine and 63g of butter)

4oz (125g) cheese (Cheddar or Cheshire or Lancashire)

4 eggs

2oz (63g) bacon (works out at 2 rashers)

2lb (1kg) meat (stewing steak, mince beef, pork, lamb, mutton, liver, kidneys, cow's heel)

1lb porridge (250g) oats

5lb (2.25kg) potatoes

1lb (250g) carrots

1lb (250g) onions (white)

2lb (1kg) green vegetables (cabbage, kale, sprouts, in winter + peas and beans, in summer)

1lb (500g) fruit (in winter = 2 small apples + 2 small pears, or plums and berries in summer)

½lb (250g) rice

1 small jar of preserves (marmalade, damson or summer fruit jam, apple or redcurrant jelly)

The irony was that rationing, which gave everyone a fair, if reduced, share of available foodstuffs, eradicated the diseases of malnutrition, which included rickets (due to lack of calcium), scurvy (due to lack of vitamin C), anaemia (due to lack of iron), vitamin deficiencies, growth retardation, etc. A hundred years on, rickets and anaemia have re-appeared to be joined by epidemics of diabetes and obesity, although this is due more to ignorance of nutrition and laziness with home cooking rather than to deprivation or lack of food supplies. The list of foodstuffs was tested by healthy adults who lived off the rations for one week in January 2015. The quality was very adequate, but the quantity left them feeling 'peckish', which is exactly what those who had to live on the rations 100 years ago said at the time. A further irony was that civilians at home ate much better than the troops at the Front, who had to rely much of the time on savoury dry biscuits, 'bully' beef (corned beef), and Machonochies rations, a thin watery stew with carrots, onions, turnips and white beans which, when heated, was just about edible, but when cold, as it often was, was termed 'a man-killer'. Folk in Bury St Edmunds probably fared better than many others in the country because there were always a few extra vegetables or a bit of extra meat for the pot. There was a noticeable lack of partridges this year, but most suspected that was because they had ended up supplementing someone's dinner. Some of the imported foreign meat was so inferior that butchers refused to sell it. There seemed to be plenty of leeks, celery, carrots, onions and turnips, and the potato crop had done well. Milk prices had risen to 3½d (about 60p) a pint (0.5 litre). The farmers were still sore about the minimum wage rates laid down for every class of worker and every bit of overtime, and complained endlessly that the retail cost of milk did not meet its wholesale production. There was actually some justification for this view, but officialdom had to step in when a few farmers threatened to send milk for cheese-making rather than for drinking because cheese was more profitable. Everything now seemed to be in short supply, even matches.

The housing situation in Bury St Edmunds and surrounding towns was becoming acute. Some of the dwellings were not fit for purpose and there was chronic overcrowding. In Bury a family of seven shared two rooms and in one of the nearby villages twelve people lived in cramped and filthy conditions in a two-bedroomed cottage. It was hoped that sensible planning and no bad placing would characterise new build. A Bill had gone before parliament seeking to increase repayment terms to eighty years for loans taken out by county councils, for dwellings to be provided by the councils and also to assist local authorities to provide decent and affordable working class housing wherever there was a need. There were endless discussions and suggestions, but nothing in Bury St Edmunds actually got done and folk knew that would be the case until the war was finally over. Then there would be urgent need for both the national and local authority housing schemes, but, for the present, it was proving to be a case of put up and shut up.

It was not exactly the land fit for heroes that had been promised. By September, 362 disabled men had returned to Bury St Edmunds and West Suffolk. Of these, 119 went back to their old jobs, 69 were unfit to work, 61 were placed with new employers, 101 were in need of light employment, and of 12 there was no trace. It was likely that they had returned to being 'gentlemen of the road', or tramps, as the more bluntly spoken put it.

A measles epidemic broke out in the autumn and reported cases of influenza were growing. By early November it was recorded that the flu outbreak was of epidemic proportions in Bury and precautions were issued by the heath authorities. Suspected sufferers should:

> ... breathe through the nose; use soap and water for washing inside of the nose; gargle each morning and evening; after sneezing they should breathe deeply; they should not wear neck mufflers; they should take regular walks; avoid crowds; ensure a warm bed; sleep with the windows open; they should not 'dope' themselves; they should avoid alcohol; and eat warm nourishing meals, especially porridge ...

These instructions could not always be followed, especially in poorer and crowded homes, and in several cases the influenza, which was an extremely virulent strain, led to pneumonia and death. Three wards at the local isolation hospital were filled with flu victims and eighteen of the first seventy-four patients died, including one of the hospital nurses.

It had originally been proposed to hold a general election in November, but the new electoral registers had taken so long to prepare that it was put back to December. Potential voters in the Bury St Edmunds parliamentary division now numbered: 11,641 men; 12,398 women; 6,718 military men; and 10 military women.

Home rule for Ireland, free trade and feminist issues were high on the agenda, and there was much excited discussion, especially among those who would be eligible to vote for the first time. Astonishingly, there were some ladies in Bury St Edmunds who did not want the vote, saying it was not a woman's place and that they preferred their husbands to deal 'with that sort of thing'. New ration books were issued and the list of shortages seemed to grow almost daily. Beer was in short supply. Butter prices were rising to 2s.6d (£6.50) per pound (500g) weight. There was talk of paraffin rationing being imminent, and a 'candle famine' was threatened. DORA lighting regulations were still in force, although there had been some relaxation, but not for Bury St Edmunds. They had learned their lesson from the Zeppelin bombings of 1915 and 1916. Zeppelin attacks had ceased altogether, but the townsfolk, still suffering from collective post-traumatic stress, were not reassured. However, there were now 'sensational rumours' about 'an important stage of the war' and that victory would not be long in coming. Many found it hard to believe after so long, but hoped, desperately, that it was true.

There seemed to be a need to focus on specific local issues rather than indications that the war might be finally nearing its end, probably due to the fact that such hopes had already been dashed a number of times. The special constables were now back in the public eye in Bury. There was concern expressed that some who had enrolled in the Volunteers would find themselves with a conflict of duty should the country be invaded. This was extremely unlikely, and had been for some time, but it didn't stop folk worrying. At another level there were more mundane issues. It had finally been decided that special constables should be provided with waterproofs and overcoats. This sentiment had been expressed early in the war, but dissident voices, lack of money due to the need to conserve funds, and the *ad hoc* provision of various bits of uniform, had lessened the impetus to take action. It was also felt they should have regulation coats and caps, as armlets were not very visible on dark nights. West Suffolk, however, had no uniform grant for the police, which was the main reason uniform provision had been scanty and why police requests for special capes and coats had not been granted.

Lists of war casualties and the work of the tribunals continued to be reported regularly, but the news now filtering through from the Fronts as October wore on was that German morale was weakening as they steadily lost ground, and there were growing demands in

Britain for the punishment of Germany and its citizens. Germany was ready to sign an armistice for peace, but US President Wilson was insisting that any peace initiatives must take account of Germany's culpability by acknowledging fourteen points:

> responsibility for the war
> invasion of Belgium
> treatment of Belgian civilians
> Zeppelin raids
> bombardment of Serbia
> submarine campaign to sink shipping
> 'war crimes' of the murders of Nurse Edith Cavell and Captain
>   Fryatt
> attacks on hospital ships
> introduction of poison gas
> illegal deportation of French and Belgian citizens
> treatment of prisoners-of-war
> deliberate destruction of an occupied country
> complicity in the Armenian massacres
> treatment of Russia

By 2 November, Turkey was out of the war, Austria was on the brink of military collapse, and the kaiser announced that he would be ready to abdicate. Finally, on 11 November, came the news the whole country had waited over four years to hear in the immortal words of David Lloyd George:

> At the eleventh minute of the eleventh hour of the eleventh month ... this morning came to end the cruellest and most terrible War that has ever scourged mankind. I hope we may say that thus, this fateful morning, came an end to all wars, hostilities ceased and the Great War came to an end.

'PEACE! End of the Great World War!' proclaimed bold black headlines in the *Bury Free Press*.

The kaiser had gone and the 'war to end all wars' was truly over. There were many local celebrations and thanksgiving services. A 'Joy Day' was held throughout West Suffolk, and there was a historic service in Bury St Edmunds cathedral followed by a torchlight procession and fireworks. The Suffolk Regiment's trophies of German guns were brought back to Bury and put on public display. There was

WW1 Roll of Honour, St Edmund's Place in Long Brackland, Bury St Edmunds.

much rejoicing, but it was tinged with sadness for all those who would not be coming back. DORA regulations were suspended and the town was a blaze of lights and bunting, but the war and the attacks by the Zeppelins had left deep scars, and there were still some Bury folk who could not bring themselves to draw back their curtains

War Memorial Angel Corner, Bury St Edmunds.

Roll of Honour for those from King Edward VI Grammar School Bury St Edmunds who made the supreme sacrifice in the Great War, St Mary's Church, Bury St Edmunds.

and let in the light. The old order had gone and a whole way of life had disappeared, but Bury St Edmunds could hold its head up with great pride in its Suffolk Regiment and for the immense contribution the town had made in so many ways to eventual victory over the Germans.

They could have had absolutely no idea that just twenty years later the same thing would happen all over again.

Index